WITHIN THE SECRET
STATE

WITHIN THE SECRET STATE

Peter Evans

Book Guild Publishing
Sussex, England

First published in Great Britain in 2009 by
The Book Guild Ltd
Pavilion View
19 New Road
Brighton, BN1 1UF

Typesetting in Times by
Keyboard Services, Luton, Bedfordshire

Printed and bound in Great Britain by
CPI Antony Rowe

A catalogue record for this book is available from
The British Library

ISBN 978 1 84624 243 4

To Matthew

Contents

Preface

For 40 years I have been watching the way the State uses power. I have seen the gradual shift in power and the take-over by a centralising bureaucracy, damaging freedoms and institutions. This inexorable change has gone on regardless of which political party was in power, although they have all been caught up in it. The British way of life is seen to be under threat from many directions. This book is intended to identify the threats, explore them and bring them to public attention.

The growth in power of the Secret State became obvious to me in my scrutiny of the Home Office for *The Times* and of MI5. Officialdom has used the development of extremism as an alibi for curbing freedoms. I was close to extremists for most of my career. I once took action which led to the identification of an associate of a major international terrorist gang; and I was hijacked by a pair of Asian fanatics, later to find a razor-sharp knife under my car seat.

The last chapter of this book will, I hope, provide a new insight into terrorism and its causes. Perhaps it may either reinforce ameliorative ideas which are beginning to emerge or provide new ones. This book is intended to be constructive, but not tamely so. In the tradition of the media going back to the Crimean War, it lives by disclosure. Because we are in a democracy, John Stuart Mill, in his great essay on liberty, said truth was the stronger for its collision with error. Thus we have an adversarial system – the two sides of Parliament and similarly in the courts of law. Some of this book will be adversarial and will not make comfortable reading.

By its own choice, MI5 – the most assertive part of the Secret State – has entered the public arena. Because of my experience in dealing with MI5 (the Security Service), I am able to assess its evolving position – its growing influence yet at the same time its vanishing mystique and its failures over the terrorist assault on Britain. This has coincided with its public entry into debate – for example about information gained by torture and whether the liberty of the subject should be curbed as a measure against terrorism. It has therefore opted to become overtly political. Dame Stella Rimington, former director general, has shown by her own revealing book how MI5 can be written about.

MI5's quiet growth in power is of intense national importance, and deserves to be examined. The targeting of innocent individuals, of which this book provides evidence, ought not to occur in a democracy, whether the victim is a prime minister, Harold Wilson, or a journalist, as the book shows. Such waywardness requires disclosure. The intelligence failure over terrorist actions is a particular reason why MI5's operations are more than ever a matter of public interest. Lives are at stake. The need to make MI5 more accountable has now been recognised. Its whole ethos, the quality of its personnel, and the way it works are vital to national security in a free society. They need to be examined. Many people have felt betrayed by a government refusal to hold a proper inquiry into the London bombings which killed 52 people.

MI5's performance can be evaluated only by understanding its nature. I provide valuable insight as an observer with an opportunity to judge attitudes and actions from close to without compromising national security or the safety of those involved in it. Now that MI5 and its tentacles figure so largely in the detaining of terrorist suspects, in spying on communities and in the law and order field it would be absurd that no-one should know by whom this is being done. In the surveillance society we need to know who is watching us. We do not want a *Stasi* in Britain.

Like any other national institution seeking to participate on its own terms in a democracy and influence decisions, the intelligence world must as a *quid pro quo* be open to understanding, evaluation, informed debate and, where needed, reform. What happens to our freedoms currently depends to a large extent on Osama Bin Laden, who is being used as an excuse for curbing them. My studies of extremist groups over 40 years have given me a unique insight into them, and I have managed to penetrate some of them. One activist I knew was hanged for murder. We need much more insight of the kind provided by Nasra Hassan into suicide bombers, cited in my last chapter. The chapter will, I hope, help to provide knowledge so that solutions can be found and we can live in greater peace.

I am grateful to my collaborators. Three of us were on *The Times* together. One of them, Michael Knipe, has worked out of more than 80 countries and been in more serious scrapes than I have. He was jailed briefly for legitimate investigation in Tanzania when I sent him there for the paper. Garry Lloyd disappeared when I despatched him to Biafra, and I was glad to get a telex eventually saying he was safe. His transport out included a dug-out canoe. Garry systematically corrected literals and other faults in my copy. I owe a great deal to them both, for encouragement, judgement, criticism and a supply of information over arduous lunches.

Others who have helped me wish to remain anonymous. I would like to thank them also, for their knowledge, wisdom, persistence, tolerance and good humour.

The forbearance of my family deserves gratitude. The whole house became an office, meal times have been dictated by the computer, and the disciplines of research and writing have dominated our lives.

Carol Biss, managing director of Book Guild Publishing, has been strong, patient and supportive, and I am also grateful to her for taking me on in the first place. Joanna Bentley is an exceptional managing editor who deserves my thanks for her skill and judgement in handling my work.

1

Enemies Within

When I accidentally fouled up an MI5 surveillance operation in Knightsbridge, London, it opened a door for me to the Secret State. The officer who introduced me to it was an old friend I had known long before he joined MI5. I did not know his job, though, and barred his way when he was in hot pursuit of his quarry. I met him afterwards and, through him, fellow officers. The insight I developed, initially into MI5, has since produced evidence of a take-over of power in Britain by forces using 'the war on terror' as an ally.

Institutions and human rights have been undermined. Safeguards to protect the independence of the police and criminal justice system are being removed. The judiciary is under attack. Increasing control by the State of key areas of British life has left military chiefs with responsibility but deprived them of the powers with which to fulfil it. If the attack on institutions were carried out by left-wing activists, it would be regarded as subversion, and MI5 would be mobilised to deal with it. Instead, MI5 is a beneficiary of this creeping coup, being an increasingly powerful part of the very State apparatus which is bringing it about.

Throughout the country there is an awareness that personal liberty is being squeezed, ostensibly as a means of state security against terrorism. However, as will become apparent in later chapters, there are darker forces at work. People's lives are being increasingly scrutinised and regulated. Protest, seen as an inconvenience, is being tamed. The harsher, more ruthless climate is epitomised by the use of torture against terror suspects and whether Britain has in any way connived at it.

As long as MI5 and successive Home Secretaries can stoke up anxiety about terrorism as a means of introducing Draconian measures, there will be little hope of relief. What Osama bin Laden is thought to achieve has a direct effect on daily life. Our way of life is being changed in his name, whether or not that is justified. Just as children were told in the Napoleonic wars that 'Boney' (Bonaparte) would get them if they didn't behave, so a new bogeyman has entered the public consciousness. The truth about Bin Laden's terrorism and the battle to combat it is of crucial importance to inroads into freedom in this country. This will be analysed later in the book.

My interest in MI5 began 40 years ago. Bustling towards me in the gutter, avoiding crowds on the pavement, was a former army officer I knew. He showed no sign of seeing me, so I stood in his path. He did not look pleased, but we agreed to meet a day or two later in a public house. He told me he was working for the Ministry of Defence, the cover MI5 people used then. He had been following someone he was watching, and I had spoilt the operation. The episode was later mentioned in an MI5 course on surveillance.

As a result of our chat, I had lunch with two of his senior colleagues and later met at the Commonwealth Club another operative who fixed up the regular delivery to me at home of papers analysing world events. They turned out to be too right wing, biased and useless, except for one paragraph describing a Soviet worry about nationalism. I used nothing of it for *The Times*.

For the following ten years I met MI5 officers regularly on a one-to-one basis, without sacrificing my professional independence. Only when I was asked by an officer to become a spy and immediately refused did our formal relationship end. Nonetheless, I have since maintained my close interest in MI5's attitudes, mores and qualities.

Evidence shows I have been targeted as a result and been put under extreme scrutiny. An ex-officer left me in no doubt about the nature of the threat. MI5 first turned against me when I refused to spy, and it realised I was not 'one of us'. Its chiefs feared I had seen too much of what it was up to. I was, after all, a journalist.

More is at stake than the existing threat to liberties, important though that is. Evidence of autocracy in Government has led others to go further. George Churchill-Coleman, who fought the IRA as head of Scotland Yard's anti-terrorist squad, famously told the *Guardian*: 'I have a horrible feeling that we are sinking into a police state, and that's not good for anybody. We live in a democracy and we should police on those standards.'[1] He was talking about the trend towards the arbitrary custody of terrorists.

He did not say we are yet in a police state, even if some of the apparatus that could be used for it is in place. But the Government has made moves towards political control of the police and the next chapter will provide facts to show that. The Government had disclosed by its actions that it wanted a state police.

Judges, upholding the rights of individuals in the clampdown against terrorism, have the precedent of a dissenting judgement by Lord Atkin in 1941 when Britain was alone against Nazi Germany and in more immediate peril than now.

> In England amidst the clash of arms the laws are not silent. They may be changed. But they speak the same language in war as in peace. It has always been one of the pillars of freedom, one of the principles of liberty for which we are now fighting, that the judges ... stand between the subject and any encroachment on his liberty by the executive, alert to see that any coercive action is justified by the law.[2]

The European Commissioner for Human Rights, Alvaro Gil-Robles, said that the introduction of control orders in Britain to detain terrorist suspects was intended to replace the ordinary criminal justice system with a parallel system run by the executive. This book will also warn against MI5's setting up parallel police across Britain. State power grows, strengthened partly – and only partly – by the need to catch terrorists.

A glaring example of take-over is the undermining of the Privy Council, which has worked with monarchs since the twelfth century. A vital part of its work is being absorbed by the bureaucracy. The change was quietly introduced in a low-key written statement on 7 March 2007 of a review by Tony Blair. 'This review determined that the functions of the Privy Council Office would be best served by becoming parts of larger Departments.'[3] Some functions would transfer to the Cabinet Office. The Department for Constitutional Affairs would get the all-important Privy Council secretariat and support for the Council's Judicial Committee. Tony Blair claimed soothingly that the Privy Council and its functions would continue unchanged.

A stinging rebuke to the Government came in the House of Lords from Lord Waddington. He said that, when the plans were leaked the previous weekend, there was considerable concern, 'not least because not so very long ago the Prime Minister tried to abolish the office of Lord Chancellor by a snap of his fingers without consulting anybody, even the Queen. Was it not high-handed to plan the abolition of the Privy Council Office without first consulting the professional bodies and universities for which it has responsibility and without consulting the Opposition...?'[4]

Baroness Amos, the Lord President of the Council, replied: 'The Privy Council Office has not been abolished. This is about a change in management structures...'

Scathing disagreement came from Lord Carey of Clifton, former Archbishop of Canterbury. He wrote in *The Times* of 28 March 2007: 'What ... I am concerned about is the way that a liberal democracy is increasingly becoming totalitarian.'[5] The changes to the Privy Council Office amounted to its virtual abolition, he said. Referring to proposals to reform the House of Lords, he added: 'Any substantial reduction or abolition of the role of bishops in the House of Lords will result in an unravelling of the Establishment of the Church of England.'

4

Peter Oborne, always alert to State subversion, wrote in his *Daily Mail* column of 10 March 2007: 'On Wednesday, practically in secret, the Prime Minister abolished the Privy Council office. The move was scarcely reported – and not even announced in the Commons.'[6]

Did the Council matter? Oborne said that the Council had been the ideal mechanism for carrying out its residual functions. A crucial role of the council is in administering the Political Honours Scrutiny Committee from whose alertness sprang, ultimately, the cash-for-honours inquiry by the Metropolitan Police. Another key function is in relation to independent public inquiries. Keeping these roles at one remove from ministerial influence is a democratic imperative, especially given the self-serving control by the State which this book describes.

Perhaps the biggest prize the executive could have would be to make the great universities of Oxford and Cambridge subservient to it. The Privy Council has safeguarded their charters. The intervention of Cambridge law academics helped to prevent the Prime Minister and executive gaining powers more suited to the monarchy before Magna Carta. This will be spelt out later in the book.

Formed to provide confidential advice to monarchs a thousand years ago – hence the word 'privy' – the council was later succeeded by the Cabinet. All Cabinet Ministers are members and four attend its monthly meetings. The Royal Family, opposition leaders and leading clergy and judges are represented on it.

Britain is suffering not only from a growth in the arbitrary power of the State but also from a shift of power, which is more sinister. The moves to politicise the police are part of this disturbing trend. It involved curbing the independence of the chief constable and bringing him or her under greater control of the Home Secretary. The dangers are obvious. Any dictator – and we are still a democracy – likes to have the police as part of the apparatus of state power: that is (partly) what a police state means. Political will enforced directly by police can lead to tyranny. The traditional separation of powers is meant to provide a chief constable with the law – and not a politician – as his guide.

The change was part of a far-reaching re-alignment of political priorities for law enforcement and intelligence agencies. Greater control over the police has to be seen against the background of greater power for MI5, already an agent of the State, and best seen as part of a usurping bureaucracy. As we shall see, MI5's growth and influence have been dramatic. *The Times* reported in January 2006: 'MI5 will soon employ twice as many counter-terrorist officers as the police, after an injection of extra money from the Treasury last month.'[7]

The question is not whether we should have spies and an organisation like MI5. We should – and given the terrorist threat, anti-terrorism measures should provide the means to prevent and defeat it. Quality is important. However, MI5 needs to be properly controlled (which it has not been), and scrutiny conducted by it, although vital against terrorism, needs to be limited only to what is essential. The furore over its failure to identify as terrorists the suicide bombers who killed 52 people in London has increased with greater knowledge of its surveillance methods.

Terrorism is currently providing an excuse for a growth of executive power, which has been taking place anyway, as in the case of the army. Like police chiefs, the heads of the armed services have also been neutered as the bureaucracy has developed. They now have less control over the destiny of those for whom they are responsible. Power has shifted away from them. Their ability to stand up to the government is thereby weakened.

General Sir Mike Jackson, who had recently retired as head of the British Army, expressed his concern at the diminution over decades of the position and authority of the three service chiefs of staff. He said on 6 December 2006 in the BBC Dimbleby lecture:

> They are seen by the public, the services themselves, the media, as responsible for all matters pertaining to the service – but this is simply not the reality. As CGS (Chief of the

General Staff), I did not hold the budget of the Army, believe it or not... Frankly, the Chiefs of Staff rather find themselves in the opposite position to that old aphorism about the ladies of the night, who are deemed to have power without responsibility. It seems to me that the chiefs have much responsibility without the power to match.[8]

General Sir Michael Rose, former head of the SAS and ex-commander of UN forces in Bosnia, was even more dismissive. British forces are so damaged by Iraq and the Blair government that they must be entirely rebuilt, he said in a *Daily Mail* interview on 12 April 2007. That could be achieved only by getting rid of the top brass who kow-towed to Whitehall, and separating decision-making from politics. The politicisation of the military was one of the most destructive developments of the Blair years. 'In recent times, the generals simply haven't spoken out and the result is that I have never seen so much confusion in the chain of command and an undermining of trust one needs from one's men.'[9]

The judges are another target for political attack. A drift towards a police state would have ominous precedents. One of the first things that a totalitarian state does is to neuter the judges and undermine traditional law. Lord Woolf, former Lord Chief Justice, called in the *Mail on Sunday* for an end to secret tribunals for terrorist suspects.[10]

The Secret State wants more power. That is what is meant when there are official warnings that some civil liberties will have to be sacrificed in the war against terrorism. Power will be transferred away from the people for their greater good.

Already the prisons had been reduced to predictable chaos by a bureaucratic take-over, destroying the disciplined service which I used to know. I have a personal plaque presented to me by the Prison Officers' Association for my coverage of its last-ditch attempt to preserve the quality of the prison service against the pressures – and disdain – being heaped upon it by civil servants who had no real idea of what they were destroying.

Doctors were also angry. The government was accused of displaying 'all the hallmarks of the very worst dictatorships' and pushing through reforms that had been 'bad news for patients', when a conference for GPs passed an overwhelming vote of no confidence in it on 14 June 2007. The conference in London by the British Medical Association[11] was against a background of what Dr Hamish Meldrum, chairman of the General Practitioners Committee, called the 'government's disastrous management of the National Health Service'. The bureaucrats had long taken it over.

As we shall see, the Government would have liked an ultimate power – in some cases to enact new laws that at present only Parliament can make. This will be detailed later in the book.

It is in the context of a drift towards autocracy that the dangers of the 'surveillance society' must be seen. Information so gained would be available to MI5, the agent of the state. But that is only part of the threat. MI5's history shows it likes power to delineate what it thinks is politically desirable – for example, through plotting by rogue agents against Harold Wilson, the smearing of people it does not like, and the past vetting of BBC staff which threatened the careers of talented broadcasters, as this book will show.

Journalists' work, especially when tiresomely independent, is scrutinised. One MI5 man I met looked puzzled. 'There is no pattern to what you write,' he said. He had been analysing the stories I had done for *The Times*. MI5 was looking for a particular line. I told him I was covering each story on its merits.

The big difference between surveillance of people in the past and now is electronic spying. There is nothing new about spying itself. 'Walls have ears' is a long familiar saying, and when I once asked Lord Denning, Master of the Rolls, where he had got a particular bit of information, he replied: 'I heard it on the grapevine.' Hiding behind the arras, as Polonius did, to overhear Hamlet would not be necessary today. A hidden microphone would do the job. The spread of eavesdropping devices and cameras has made the British people some of the most spied upon in the world.

MI5 and GCHQ, with the help of 'echelon', the international

eavesdropping technology, can pick and choose what they want to know, given reasonable suspicion. But what is reasonable? Tracking the movement of cars and people will be supplemented by the monitoring of telephone calls, e-mails and the study by MI5 of what topics people are interested in. Your secrets will be known.

Centralised electronic records, whether held by the National Health Service or other organisations, can intrude upon the privacy of the patient or customer and make the job of spying easier. Individual threats to liberty may be known by the informed but it is not until they are added up (see Chapter 8), that their full impact is apparent. We are not only a much spied-upon people, but also a 'processed' people and we are in danger of being controlled.

I take it for granted that my e-mails and phone calls are scrutinised, given the insider knowledge I have about intrusion into communications and my inquiries into the secret state. I will reveal firm evidence of this phone-tapping later in the book. And if such surveillance is happening to me, it is also happening to other people.

The trouble is that we are in the middle of an electronic stand-off with the terrorists, and bugging systems need to be used against them. This begs the question as to who is really a threat, even among the freedom-loving native British, and here MI5's judgement has sometimes been disastrously wrong in wasting money on the wrong targets – myself and others like me, for example – or failing to spot the right ones.

Spin-doctoring, an arm of despotic government, took us to war in Iraq. Opposition counted for nothing. Alan Greenspan, the leading Republican economist for a generation, says in his memoir: 'I am saddened that it is politically inconvenient to acknowledge what everyone knows: the Iraq war is largely about oil.' Greenspan, now retired, was writing in *The Age of Turbulence: Adventures in a New World*.[12] The British and US governments have not the credibility to counter, as they should, the terrorists' propaganda over Iraq, Afghanistan, Lebanon and the Israelis. The terrorists believe that America's war is itself terrorist, and it has encouraged a deadly reaction by them to it. Britain and America are targets for the terrorists. The 'axis of evil' consists, from their perverted propaganda viewpoint, of Britain and the United States. This does not mean that the terrorists are right. They are evil. But we need right on our side, and Blair and Bush have not provided this convincingly enough. Terrorism has presented an excuse for a curbing of liberties in favour of illiberal restrictions.

Too many young Muslims in Britain feel alienated. There are no 'new' Muslims in the sense that there is New Labour, disentangling itself from its past. Some Muslims may not observe traditions as strictly as others, but that is true of people in all religions, and at heart Muslims are firm in their basic beliefs. In many ways they set an admirable example in our dehumanising society. President Bush made an insensitive reference to the crusades which still after a thousand years arouse Muslim anger. British policies have already provided the excuse for bombing here.

If British foreign policy further alienates Muslims here, this will be seen as an excuse to make further inroads into liberties and for spying against our people. For the Government to be tough on terror means it should be tough on itself – and not engage in reckless enterprises. If foreign policy had been as cautious at the time as Gordon Brown's economic policy, there would have been no inflation of terrorism and we would be living within our security means.

My experience of the secret world has shown it to be lamentably slow in picking up trends. The intelligence analysts have failed repeatedly. Preachers of hate were allowed to flourish in Britain in the 1990s and immediately afterwards for too long. The fault is not new. Throughout the 1970s I was warning about a forthcoming clash on a grand scale between young black people and police, but the MI5 men I met showed only indifference. The symptoms did not fit with their preconceptions. The riots flared. More subtle insights seemed to be beyond them. As with all bureaucracies, originality of thought is not welcomed by run-of the-mill intelligence officers. They are stuck in a groove.

The terrorist outrages which cause such havoc are the destructive waves on the surface. These MI5 likes to chase after as they break on the shore. What matters more are the great, powerful currents underneath which give rise to them and can change our lives. The huge forces which gave rise to the Tupamaros in South America, the row over Scottish independence, the Biafran War, the ethnic cleansing following the break-up of Yugoslavia and the falling apart of Soviet Russia are not entirely disparate. The immediate triggers may be different, but they involve similar characteristics, as we shall see.

Black power, like Islamist terrorism, is an example. It is a startling fact that, long before the suicide bombing of America by Islamist terrorists, Black Power activists were saying they wished to put out the eye of the capitalist octopus in London and New York. This I reported in an article for the University College of Wales, Aberystwyth, on the 'root of nationalism', in 1975. The Black Power activists were speaking rhetorically and not with the murderous intent of the (later) Islamist terrorists. The terrorists carried out their own, similar wish.[13] On 14 March 2007 a German expert on Islamic fundamentalism, Dr Matthias Kuntzel, was due to discuss similarities between the Nazis and Islamist extremists at Leeds University. But the meeting was called off for security reasons. According to the university, not enough time was given to prepare for it.

Islamists would object to the comparison, which would be offensive to them. They regard themselves as self-evidently different. The Third Reich was born out of a defeated Germany. The present support for Bin Laden comes from the bombing of Lebanon, the aggression of Israel and the bloody aftermath of the invasion of Iraq. Hitler intimidated with Stuka dive bombers. Al-Qaeda has killed hostages. Hitler wanted purity of race. Al-Qaeda seeks purity of religion. The blitz is invoked by Londoners under attack once more from bombs, this time from Islamist extremists, as a symbol of historic resistance. They have one thing directly in common though. Hitler sought to eliminate the Jews, and al-Qaeda wants an end to Israel.

The surge in Islamist power provokes Government reactions.

This in turn influences the extent to which inroads can be made into our liberal society and the institutions which safeguard it. We need to know where the extremism comes from. The next chapter will show how the drive for dominance by the Secret State involves a bid to control the police and change the nature of its relationship with the public.

2

The Police Under Threat

The progress of the government take-over of the police can be measured.
The starting point is one of Britain's most famous legal statements,
proclaiming the independence of the police from political control. It
was made with ringing authority by Lord Denning, Master of the Rolls,
in 1968, and has since resounded around the world. The words of Lord
Denning cited here have been widely reprinted, as in the annual report
for 2005 of the Central Bureau of Investigation under the Government
of India,[1] which I quote here. Because the judgement is fundamental
to democracy and freedoms in Britain – freedoms now being put in
jeopardy – here is an extract in full. Lord Denning said:

I have no hesitation in holding that, like every constable in
the land, he (the Police Commissioner) should be, and is,
independent of the executive. He is not subject to the orders
of the Secretary of State, save that under the Police Act 1964,
the Secretary of State can call upon him to give a report, or
retire in the interests of efficiency.

I hold it to be the duty of the Commissioner of Police of
the Metropolis, as it is of every chief constable, to enforce
the law of the land. He must take steps so to post his men
that crimes may be detected; and that honest citizens may go
about their affairs in peace. He must decide whether or not
suspected persons are to be prosecuted; and, if need be, bring
the prosecution or see that it is brought.

13

But in all these things he is not the servant of anyone, save the law itself. No Minister of the Crown can tell him that he must, or must not, keep observation on this place or that; or that he must, or must not, prosecute this man or that one.

Nor can any police authority tell him so. The responsibility for law enforcement lies on him. He is answerable to the law and the law alone.

The case which gave rise to the ruling was brought by Raymond Blackburn who first approached *The Times*, complaining that he wished the Metropolitan police to enforce gaming laws properly. With my backing as UK news editor, the story was taken up by Norman Fowler, who was then home affairs correspondent and is now Lord Fowler, a former cabinet minister and Conservative Party chairman. Blackburn came to *The Times* again in 1973 and saw me, now home affairs correspondent. This time he alleged that the police were not enforcing the law against pornography. His case was rejected but, as in 1968, the courts left the way open for intervention by judges if the refusal of the police to enforce the law was serious enough.

The 1968 ruling which ensued from those initiatives has echoes today with threats to the police of control by the State. The chief constable should not have to follow politicians' *diktats*, otherwise the force would cease to be the police of the people, or civilians in uniform, which is how they have been traditionally regarded. They would instead become more like the armed services and creatures of government, part of a feared drift towards a police state.

Yet this change is happening, and it goes against Lord Denning's ruling. One sign was the establishment in July 2006 of a new body which gave the Home Secretary the chance to interfere in policing. The National Policing Board oversees 'the Home Secretary's annual national strategic priorities for policing'. It will, of course, be argued with a comforting smile, that this is not unconstitutional. Once the precedent of ministerial interference is established, however,

14

political priorities could make the police do the Government's bidding.

John Reid, who resigned as Home Secretary in May 2007, suffered a significant set-back to his plans, but you have to dig into the minutes of the National Policing Board to find it.[2] The assault on police independence seemed nicely predictable at its meeting on 28 November 2006 when Mr Reid said a key task for the Board was to agree the priorities for the police against the backdrop of his review of the Home Office and criminal justice system. The Board would want to keep a close eye on progress in implementing the various elements of police reform.

The next stage of the plan towards a state police was to be a 'vision' document to 'set a 3–5 year horizon for the police service and to support the National Policing Board in setting priorities. It should focus on policing rather than the wider community safety agenda.' The minutes showed the police were 'broadly content with the way that the vision was being taken forward'. They were in discussion with members, 'and would provide comments to the Home Office'.

Suddenly the police woke up. The Home Secretary, chairing the Board's meeting on 17 January 2007, did not get his way – then, at least. The Association of Chief Police Officers (ACPO) said they would have difficulty in signing up to a vision in the proposed timescale as they were awaiting the outcome of their own work on future matters due in April/May. The police obviously expected to have a vision of their own future. The minutes added: 'Given that, Ministers had decided that a short statement of values should be issued as a Home Office document.' It was a tactical defeat for John Reid. A 'short statement of values' is not the same as a 'vision' under the chairmanship of the Home Secretary. Whether a new Home Secretary puts the police in harness will be constitutionally important.

As Lord Denning said of the Metropolitan Police Commissioner: 'He ... should be, and is, independent of the executive. He is not subject to the orders of the Secretary of State, save that under the

15

Police Act 1964, the Secretary of State can call upon him to give a report, or retire in the interests of efficiency.'

The most startling and immediate example of State power over law enforcement was the decision to call off a major investigation by the Serious Fraud Office into a £6 billion defence deal with Saudi Arabia, which was reported to be threatening to pull out of it. The House of Lords later ruled the decision lawful. On 14 December 2006 Lord Goldsmith, the Attorney General, stated that the decision had been taken in the wider public interest, which had to be balanced against the rule of law. He thought that a prosecution could not be brought. Tony Blair and Des Browne, the Defence Secretary, had argued that carrying on the investigation would harm intelligence and diplomatic co-operation with Saudi Arabia, thus damaging the UK's national security. Ministerial interference in law enforcement was thus sanctioned – a massive constitutional shift. Opponents called it 'scandalous'. If this is the point of principle that now holds sway, there is no official barrier to other political pressure on the police, the agents of law enforcement, if it is regarded as in the national interest. Anti-terrorism is in the national interest and thus would provide an overwhelming reason for interference. The Serious Fraud Office investigation would, however, go on in five countries.[3]

There are even more explosive implications, this time involving Lord Goldsmith's advice over the legality of the Iraq war. On 7 March 2003 he noted possible legal arguments that might be made against the war. He said there were 'a number of ways' in which legal action could be brought by the war's opponents. 'We cannot be certain they would not succeed,' he said. A solution might be a second UN resolution. There were questions as to whether the wording of previous resolutions on Iraq authorised military action. The advice of 7 March was not shown to the Cabinet.

Three days before the war started, Lord Goldsmith's further advice *was* shown to the Cabinet. In a written answer to Parliament on 17 March he had no doubts, stating: 'Authority to use force against Iraq exists from previous UN resolutions.' The question now arises whether the wider public interest and national security in any way influenced his changed later ruling, as it did later over the Saudi arms deal investigation.

'The wider public interest and national security' are handy nostrums for a controlling government to use. They would justify a further threat to police independence in enforcing the law. It comes from Whitehall's new power against terrorism, reinforced by machinery introduced by John Reid on 29 March 2007. He would chair a weekly strategic meeting and the Prime Minister would chair a security committee monthly. If desired this could provide opportunity for political influence over operations.

The inspirational anti-terrorist police chief, Peter Clarke, could well have found his clear and decisive leadership subjected to political committee-think in the future. He stepped down from his job in a surprise move in September 2007. It would be naïve to think the police would be allowed to get on and do their job without interference. This would be inevitable since the police have become part of new anti-terrorist machinery. With more people already privy to secret operations these have already been jeopardised by leaks. Mr Clarke believed that leaks, from whatever source, were putting lives at risk. Leaking in the wrong circumstances could be a criminal offence, a sanction the police have available.

Coinciding with a speech by John Reid about his new anti-terrorist policy, Mr Clarke's complaint about leaks could not have been more timely. He said (24 April 2007) that people providing off-the-record briefings should be 'thoroughly ashamed'. He added:

What I am talking about is the deliberate leaking of highly sensitive operational intelligence, often classified, and the unauthorised release of which can be a criminal offence.

I make no allegations about the source of the leaks or about individual cases. What is clear is that there are a number, a small number I am sure, of misguided individuals who betray confidences.

Perhaps they look to curry favour with certain journalists

17

or to squeeze out some short-term presentational advantage. I do not know what motivates them. The people who do this either do not know or do not care what damage they do.

If they do know, then they are beneath contempt. If they do not know, then let me tell them: they compromise investigations, they reveal sources of life-saving intelligence, in the worst cases they put lives at risk. I wonder if they simply do not care.[4]

Some suspected the leaks could be a form of spin-doctoring. Tony Blair rejected demands for an enquiry into them. David Cameron, the Conservative leader, and the Liberal Democrats had both called for an investigation. The latest dispute follows police denials of responsibility for leaks about the cash for honours inquiry which had caused wide concern, not least in Downing Street.

Mr Clarke's wide-ranging speech also coincided with an announcement that Jonathan Evans, the new head of MI5, had on the same day briefed the Prime Minister and Cabinet colleagues at the first meeting of the Government's committee on security and terrorism. Peter Clarke was equally well-equipped to assess al-Qaeda's potential, if not more so. Police work, even more than MI5's, is anchored firmly in the demands of the criminal law.

The Whitehall establishment was accused of leading the police astray in a disastrous anti-terror raid, on 2 June 2006, against alleged suspects at Forest Gate, east London. Senior officials, ministers and intelligence insiders were said to be involved in the decision to act, which was based on faulty intelligence by MI5.

This view conflicts with the subsequent official line that the police made the operational decision on the basis of carefully tested intelligence; and that the police were not let down by MI5 – there was joint working. The relationship between police and MI5 was officially explained in a BBC Radio 4 programme about 'the real spooks' (11 December 2007).

The fiasco caused Asian-led protests against police. Al-Qaeda, in its search for British recruits, must have been delighted. The

Observer reported on 11 June 2006: 'Scotland Yard warned MI5 it had serious reservations about the credibility of the source whose information triggered the Forest Gate anti-terrorism raid only hours before police stormed the suspects' house in East London.'[5]

More than 250 police officers were controversially involved in the 4 a.m. raid after an informant wrongly claimed that there was a chemical device at the property for use in a terrorist attack. One of two brothers later detained was shot as police burst in. They found no chemical device and later apologised for the 'hurt' they had caused the brothers who were cleared of suspicion and released without charge. The outcome was doubly embarrassing because the police were also facing inquiries over the fatal shooting in London of an innocent Brazilian wrongly suspected of being a terrorist.

Jimmy Burns, the *Financial Times* security specialist, disclosed (11 June 2006) that the raid took place after ministers and officials were advised by MI5 that a device involving cyanide was being prepared and that urgent action was necessary to protect public safety. 'According to Whitehall and police insiders, a series of meetings and consultations involving senior officials and ministers was held before the raid in Forest Gate, east London.'[6]

Ken Livingstone, London's mayor, said he had read about allegations in the *Observer*. 'This is very worrying indeed,' he said on the BBC Radio 4 Today programme, 'because I think Londoners are prepared to accept that the Commissioner of Police has the right to initiate these sorts of raids, has the power and responsibility. We have always worked on the basis that they are free from political interference.'[7] Lord Denning would have agreed with him.

The shooting of Mohammed Abdul Kahar at Forest Gate had dire consequences which could have been even worse. Anyone who has ever fired a weapon knows the sensitivity required with the finger on the trigger. Illustrations of the kind of protective suit worn by the marksman in Forest Gate make it obvious that his finger could not possibly have been as sensitive on the trigger as it would otherwise have been, through no fault of his own. Because the chemicals were wrongly stated to be found in the house,

19

protective suits with two further layers and a respirator had to be worn. Two gloves on each hand – a cotton under-glove and rubber over-glove – would have prevented the sense of touch any marksman prefers. To make handling more difficult, the Heckler & Koch MP5 carbine has, like other guns, a guard round the trigger. Given the intelligence police were fed, the safety catch would presumably have had to be off. Not surprisingly, the Independent Police Commission concluded that the weapon went off by accident and that the marksman should not face criminal charges or disciplinary procedures.

Had proper respect been given to the skills and experience of the police Special Branch, such a mistake might not have been made. But long-standing rivalry between the police and MI5 had resulted in the eclipse of the Special Branch. It had begun with the determination of Stella Rimington, then chief of MI5, to give her agency the lead in fighting terror. The Special Branch lost the battle. Kenneth Clarke, Home Secretary, announced in 1992 that MI5 was to do as Rimington wished. The lead was hers.

Now the balance is swinging the other way. Intelligence failures over the London bombing and Forest Gate have exposed MI5's weaknesses. Whatever the accuracy of intelligence concerning an alleged plot, disclosed on 10 August 2006, to down airliners over the Atlantic, there was no doubt this time that the police took the lead. Scotland Yard references to it being a criminal investigation put it firmly in the anti-terrorist squad's court. By nature circumspect, Peter Clarke, the Yard's anti-terrorist squad chief, made vividly plain on 21 August 2006 the huge amount of work the police had to do. There had so far been some 69 searches in houses, flats, business premises, vehicles and open spaces. As well as bomb-making equipment 'we have found more than 400 computers, 200 mobile telephones and 8,000 items of removable storage media such as memory sticks, CDs and DVDs.'[8] All the data would be analysed over many months.

More credit was given to the police when a British Muslim admitted plotting to build a radio-active 'dirty bomb' and carry

out a series of attacks in Britain.[9] Dhiren Barot was jailed for life
– a minimum of 40 years, later reduced to 30 years on appeal.[10]
Edmund Lawson, QC for the prosecution, told Woolwich Crown
Court that Barot plotted to attack the International Monetary Fund
and World Bank in Washington, the New York Stock Exchange
and Citigroup buildings in New York, and the Prudential building
in Newark. Mr Lawson said that Barot had admitted planning
terrorist murders in the US and Britain.[11] The court heard that
details were found on Barot's computer of a project to detonate in
Britain three limousines packed with gas cylinders and explosives
in underground car parks. The prosecution said Barot's plans were
not at an advanced stage – he had no funding, vehicles or bomb-
making equipment. Mr Lawson said the so-called 'dirty bomb' plot
was unlikely to kill anyone. Ian Macdonald QC, representing Barot,
also said that the radiation plot had not been intended to kill.[12]
The *Daily Mail* reported Scotland Yard's success in August 2004
when Barot, a banker's son and al-Qaeda leader, was arrested in
Harlesden, north-west London.[13] He admits conspiracy to murder.

The police success came after a period of mixed fortunes for
them. The defeat of the Special Branch has been followed by its
end as a separate entity, but it has been rescued in a merger with
the anti-terrorist branch, where its skills and experience will be
invaluable. Unlike MI5, it is streetwise. Police begin their training
on the streets. They know people. Officers have to face cross-
examination regularly in court and, unlike MI5, are publicly
accountable. By contrast, the absence of criticism gives MI5 an
overweening confidence that what it believes to be the case really
is so and will happen. The Forest Gate debacle was a result. Special
Branch officers are professional sceptics.

MI5 and the police are officially said to be co-operating closely.
Dean Godson, research director of the Policy Exchange think tank,
wrote in *The Times* (23 August 2007) that Jonathan Evans, head of
MI5, went to see Sir Paul Scott-Lee, the West Midlands chief constable,
to urge him to reorder his force priorities – and devote more resources
to the 'sexier' topic of counter-terrorism. Evans's reported comments

show a new urgency to put terrorism, the dangers of which he is acutely aware, higher on the national agenda. But what would Lord Denning, defender of police operational independence, have thought? Godson says that Sir Paul is his own man.[14]

Another idea pushed by MI5 was that in tracking suspected or known Islamist extremists, police should employ techniques used against paedophiles. They should collate sightings of extremists and note whom they met and which areas they frequented (something police would do anyway).

However, these ideas were flawed, as *The Times* showed (16 April 2007). High up in the story we read: '*Thousands* of police officers on the beat in areas with large Pakistani communities – such as Birmingham, Leeds and London – will be *expected* to keep a look-out for young Muslims known to have become radicals' (my italics).[15] It turned out that was not the case. Embarrassingly for MI5, it could not tell the police what to do. The story continued: 'The security sources later added that it was a matter for individual police forces to decide how to prioritise their resources in keeping track of Islamic extremists.' The climb-down would have pleased Lord Denning. Chief constables are responsible to the law, not to MI5. MI5 evidently did not realise that Muslims require different treatment. Unlike paedophiles, extremists have a terrorist organisation to turn to when angered by pressure and, if the police failed to appreciate the difference, they would simply become al-Qaeda's recruiting sergeant.

The official line given in the BBC Radio 4 programme about 'the real spooks' is that the police and the Security Service are now closely integrated in their anti-terrorist operations. The late Mike Todd, Manchester's chief constable, said: 'When you look at the link between the service and the police, it reaches literally from the director general of the security service, the chief constable, right the way down to a community police officer, working in one of our communities.' This, of course, raises questions about the autonomy, separate identity and accountability of the police.

The official view is that communities would be only too glad to know watch was being kept against terrorism. But a BBC investigation found British Muslims who believed they had been put under pressure to inform on their own communities. The intelligence services deny that they pressurise people into becoming informants.[16] (See also Chapter 4.)

Eight thousand suspected al-Qaeda sympathisers were already being scrutinised by MI5 with the help of its regional centres and GCHQ. It was acting on surveys which had shown that between 5 and 7 per cent of British Muslims thought the London bombings were justified. As we shall see later in the book, a more recent poll by the Gallup Organisation has disclosed that nine out of ten Muslims in London believed attacks that targeted civilians were unjustified and morally wrong. The findings called into question current security policy, but not the need to protect the public.

The increasing dominance of MI5 was, however, being matched by proposals to produce within the police their own anti-terrorist force across the country. The plan was recommended by Her Majesty's Inspectorate of Constabulary, which in recent years has figured more in strategy making than used to be the case. Denis O'Connor, a former chief constable of Surrey and an assistant commissioner at Scotland Yard, envisaged a new chief counter-terrorism co-ordinator leading up to ten freshly created regional specialist squads. Some could have up to 50 officers. Being police, and not MI5, they would have a more direct input from community-conscious local constabularies about embryonic threats. The combination of community policing and high-calibre anti-terrorist officers, as envisaged by the plan, would provide the police with the sort of clout that a democracy encourages and allows – but which is also answerable to the public. Moreover it had a better chance of involving the public, which MI5, being a State agency, cannot overtly do. Peter Clarke was national co-ordinator for operations. As well as Greater Manchester's larger unit, others were being formed in West Midlands, West Yorkshire and London. They would have a chance of matching MI5's regional development.

Nor did the police intend to be sidelined by the creation of another rival body – the Serious Organised Crime Agency (SOCA), the so-called 'British FBI'. *The Sunday Times* reported on 23 July 2006 that Lord Goldsmith was to announce proposals for a national fraud squad 'to tackle organised crime and to choke off funding for terrorists'.[17] This raised an intriguing question: wasn't this supposed to be part of the job of the Serious Organised Crime agency (SOCA)? 'Organised crime' figures in SOCA's title. The chairman is Sir Stephen Lander, MI5's former boss. SOCA has been caricatured as the Home Secretary's private police force – the Government's force. The new fraud squad is a counter to it, depending more on down-to-earth traditional policing. SOCA, with its huge powers, is less accountable to the public than the new squad is.

The operational autonomy of the police, like that of the armed services and even of the judiciary, is under threat, as we have seen. A bureaucratic coup has happened before, with a disastrous take-over of the prison service in the 1960s. It has been in perpetual crisis ever since. I wrote in 1980: 'The confusion and loss of morale which have helped to bring the Prison Service to the brink of disaster were predicted as long ago as 1963 by opponents of Whitehall's successful attempts, made then and subsequently, to gain bureaucratic power over the prison system.'

Just as leaders of the armed services, the police and judges today face threats to their autonomy, so then did the prison service. Nowhere was this subversion by the bureaucracy spelt out more clearly than by Henry Brooke, the then Home Secretary. The much respected Prison Commission, which supervised the running of the jails, was abolished. Brooke said on 3 February 1963: 'Constitutionally it is anomalous and misleading that the Commission should appear to be a separate and independent body.'[18]

Today it may also be anomalous and misleading to the power-hungry bureaucracy that the police, judges and the armed services, should appear to be separate and independent bodies. Pressure on the judges has become more apparent. John Reid, when Home Secretary, had shown his willingness to order police about when he should not have done. The police will not accept orders from ministers. They are not their political masters. Chief officers jumped on a statement by John Reid that 440 police officers would be seconded to hunt down disappeared illegal immigrants. In a communiqué to chief officers, Ken Jones, ACPO's president, said that the press release with the announcement 'was not shown to ACPO and would not have been endorsed'.[19]

The deviousness with which the Prison Service was taken over should alert other national institutions. They need to keep a close eye on bodies which are introduced ostensibly to help them but could turn out eventually to dominate them. The Police Standards Unit is one. It exists to provide 'intensive support to police forces and basic command units to help them meet the desired level of performance'. In other words, it advises them what to do. What happens if the advice is not followed is not clear. Thinking long term, as always, the bureaucracy could well be plotting how to turn advice into instructions. It would be a convenient alternative to direct control over a national force, when this was not possible for the time being. The increasing use of computer links also provided an opportunity for the bureaucracy to fiddle in police business.

Now another body has been flexing its muscles – the National Policing Improvement Agency which has arrived with as fine an example of bureaucratic gobbledegook as any in Whitehall's lexicon:

Police buy-in will be a feature of the NPIA because the service will be involved in all aspects of the agency's work from membership of the NPIA board and programme boards to the involvement of police business experts in delivering programmes. The NPIA will be a truly police owned and led body. The agency will develop a more professional business change capability for the service, forging a strong link between the delivery of information and communications technology support and overall business change programmes. ICT delivery will be just one enabler for improving the way forces work.[20]

'The copper on the beat', as we used to say, must be wonderfully enthused by such alien language. As with staff in hospitals and schools, the constable is struggling to do the job for which he is trained – serving the public. He or she is becoming a bureaucrat in uniform rather than simply a civilian in uniform. Jan Berry, chair of the Police Federation, said the Government was obsessed with targets and data collection.[21] A dossier drawn up by the Federation showed officers were having to meet Government targets by making 'ludicrous' arrests for trivialities. It included a man cautioned for being 'in possession of an egg with intent to throw', and two children arrested for being in possession of a toy pistol. Jan Berry said: 'We have police officers who are considering leaving the service over this because it is not the job they signed up to do . . . Just talking to people and giving them a few words of advice cannot be counted as easily as a ticket. But sometimes it is just as effective as taking someone to court.' Police fear that being driven not to use their powers of discretion will distance them from the public and lose support. Traditionally the power of discretion – possibly the greatest an officer has – has enabled them to keep the peace without fuss.

David Cameron, the Conservative leader, said in July 2006 that less than a fifth of an officer's time was spent on the beat. A Home Office study in 2005 found that only 1 per cent of police time was spent on proactively reducing crime – the main point of policing. One officer told Cameron: 'It takes at least six hours to deal with an arrest. If it's a complex case – much, much longer. If a normal, regular PC makes an arrest they will not see the streets again on that tour of duty.'[22]

In June 2006 Ken Jones, president of the Association of Chief Police Officers, said: 'We need to restore the ability of cops on the street to enforce the law in an efficient and effective way. It's got horribly bureaucratic, horribly formulaic and Byzantine.'[23] The police are in danger of losing their sense of purpose. Evidence from prisons shows that revision of the old structure of command has undermined what used to be called a disciplined service. Prisons were run like ships. Just as admirals are now not so free to lead, so prisons are heavily barnacled with bureaucracy.

The 'War on Terror', as it used to be called, has constables as foot soldiers. We are only on the way to perhaps being a police state, but the Government would already like us to have state police. As a result of terrorism, more police carry arms. Laws initiated by Tony Blair are now more restrictive. In carrying them out, the police are also being restrictive, and sometimes oppressively so, at the government's bidding. Criticism of police is a result, further alienating them from the public. Controversial stop-and-search powers were used to detain Walter Wolfgang, an 82-year old peace protester, when he was removed from the 2005 Labour Party conference after shouting 'nonsense' at Jack Straw, then Foreign Secretary. We may not yet be in a police state, but the way the law is carried out these days allows protesters to claim that Britain is on the verge of becoming one.

If the government is abrasive it is the police who collect the abrasions, as they did in the miners' strike with the Government's battle to destroy the power of the National Union of Mineworkers. Douglas Hurd, the then Home Secretary, told me at the time police tactics were an operational matter with which he was not involved. The present moves to allow the Home Secretary to set strategic targets for the police indicate a constitutional change. Concern about the effect on the nature of British policing is felt in all ranks. Jan Berry, chair of the Police Federation, which represents officers up to the rank of chief inspector, was outspoken in defending forces' independence. She said that, while as servants of the Crown police officers had been traditionally independent of politicians, 'control of the police is gradually but surely being centralised and politicised'.[24]

All is made easier by a technological revolution which has changed the way police work and made centralised control easier. That control the Government would like to get its hands on.

The information and control systems on which the police depend need to be efficient and properly co-ordinated, but a side-effect can be to dehumanise policing. Over-centralised control has devalued important traditional concepts which have provided continuity and identity. The police force is an organism not a mechanism, and its traditions are its nervous system. It is tribal. I found for my book *The Police Revolution* that an astonishing number of officers were from families in which fathers, grandfathers, uncles, brothers and sisters had also served in the police.[25]

The beginning of law enforcement by the police tribe is knowing what to praise and blame. Police jargon expressed it. 'Snow drop', used in Scotland, described the kinky theft of women's underwear from a clothes line. Some of the language reflects police attitudes which are part of the organic nature of the force. A policeman who didn't put himself about was 'a uniform carrier'. Hippies and tramps were at one stage called 'slag'. A corner-cutting CID officer was known as 'swift'. Police don't like a show-off as a colleague and said he was 'putting himself about'. Graduates at the Police College were sometimes called 'five day wonders'. 'Clever talk' is not appreciated.

These are all traits traditional police have not liked. If one thinks of the opposite of these terms, it gives an idea of what they do like. The opposite of a uniform carrier is someone conscientious. The opposite of slag is someone of value to society. Someone who proceeds slowly and methodically to get a job well done within the regulations is the opposite of swift. Not for nothing has the traditional bobby been called 'Pc Plod'.

This organism called the police force cannot easily be ordered about. Police are not like soldiers. They can work as a team, march about during training, salute and may have a semi-military appearance, but they are not yet a state police. Most of the strength of the police force is from the bottom up, not from the top down, and the individual constable is his own man (or woman).

The beginning of 2007 saw a re-assertion by police of their independence. The so-called 'cash for honours' investigation was one sign that, whatever John Reid might have said about laying down priorities for the police, they would still see those priorities in terms of the law and not of political aims. The Crown Prosecution

Service said after a 16-month police inquiry there was insufficient evidence to 'provide a realistic prospect of conviction against any individual for any offence in relation to this matter'.[26] Police also resisted a £1 billion plan for force mergers, called off in July 2006. An inspector of constabulary said that many forces could not meet the needs of modern policing because they were too small. Tony McNulty, the policing minister, said mergers would not be imposed as planned because most forces had objected and a way to pay for the changes had not been found.

A national force would be easier for the Government to take over. The chief constable of a national force would no longer be the local bobby with the county or city as his beat. The identity of the police would be confused and threatened. Pride in the service would suffer. The quirky sense of duty which distinguishes the individual police officer would not be as easy to encourage or manage. Officers who do not like one force can nowadays join another, and Britain would have a state police.

Whitehall had lost the argument, for the time being at least. But the lessons of the past fifty years have shown that it will not give up. The 'state police' is, for Labour, a concept very much alive.

The police are also under threat from the Tories. David Cameron shows a good bedside manner when he makes his diagnosis of the police but the cure may be worse than the illness. Elected commissioners would be able to sack inadequate police chiefs (and one wonders who is to judge their quality). The independence of the chief constable would be compromised, perhaps to win votes. The Conservatives want better co-operation between constabularies or a single national force, which would inevitably be easier to control politically, from the top down.

The way that MI5 has moved into the driving seat of anti-terrorist strategy will be shown in the next chapter. The police are making up lost ground with their new regional anti-terror teams. Each has about 350 staff and will link with security services. They will do what police are good at and which the community wants – investigate suspects by focusing on potential law-breaking by terrorists.

3

The Security Services Win Power

The Government has encouraged MI5's dash for power. In the defence of the realm it has been given a free hand. Greater control by the state over the police and armed forces showed that the balance of advantage was altering.

Backing for the Security Services has already resulted in a succession of quiet take-overs:

- An MI5 man chairs the 'British FBI' with unprecedented clout.
- An MI5 man heads security in Parliament with Draconian powers.
- MI5 is developing eight spying centres across Britain.
- A plan, which failed, attempted to tap MPs' telephones.

Of course, everything must be done to defeat terrorism and serious crime, and by themselves such measures might well be acceptable. In November 2006 MI5 claimed to know of some 30 plots and 1,600 people involved in them – an obvious plea for more money and staff. But MI5 and its partners link with each other like nerve cells and deal in power as well as information. MI5 has worked closely with Sir Stephen Lander, the chairman of SOCA, the heavyweight Serious Organised Crime Agency, who is himself a former director of MI5. The link creates opportunity for massive transfer of intelligence without adequate supervision. Newly

31

created provincial spying centres form part of the network, linking also with SOCA. Since MI5 will work closely with both its provincial networks and with SOCA, it would be naïve to think it does not therefore work closely with its placeman covering Parliament, moved in to head security.[1] He has real power and must surely, even in the ordinary run-of-the-mill, day-to-day business in the House, hear something about MPs, even if their telephones are not, for the moment, to be tapped.

MI5 has not been properly answerable, except to a weak and ineffective Intelligence and Security Committee. MI5 and its off-shoots have lacked the accountability that the police have. It seeks to avoid rigorous scrutiny by those it regards as outsiders and who are difficult to influence. All wars provide opportunity for the ambitious, and this one, against terrorism, has helped MI5 in its unprecedented pursuit of growth, power and influence, alongside a genuine need to have enough resources to cope with a terrorist threat of a kind and origin unknown before in Britain.

MI5's recent history shows its method of expansion. The strategy is to place its personnel in new posts. The Serious Organised Crime Agency (SOCA) has been handed MI5's previous task of tackling serious crime. MI5 was involved in that when the Cold War came to an end and it otherwise had less to do. It has been criticised for allowing itself to be distracted at the time – the 1990s – from tackling the hate preachers and future Islamist extremists under their influence.

Like al-Qaeda internationally, MI5 has developed a network nationally. SOCA, the new agency, has taken over major crime busting bodies – the National Criminal Intelligence Service (NCIS); the National Crime Squad; work by HM Revenue and Customs against serious drug trafficking and to recover criminal gains; and the Home Office staff fighting immigration crime gangs. Thus MI5 is firmly connected to a law and order alliance, which seems formidable but on examination is seen to be flawed, as will be shown.

Since MI5 has relinquished its own crime-fighting role, the need for a helpful relationship with SOCA, ostensibly a crime fighter, is not so pressing, except for intelligence reasons. In the words of the cliché, knowledge is power, and intelligence is a major part of SOCA's role. Constraints imposed in Parliament to guard against terrorists may be a taste of things to come. The man from MI5 can order the Prime Minister, the Cabinet and MPs out of the chamber or keep them there, if need be, in the event of a major terrorist emergency.[2] Lord Goldsmith, the Attorney General, was not pleased when he was confronted by locked doors in Westminster during an anthrax scare. He was reported in the *Mail on Sunday* as saying: 'You are preventing me from doing my departmental and government duties. This is ridiculous.'[3] One of the most powerful figures in government, he was for the time rendered powerless, and his frustration and embarrassment were the result of measures following the appointment there of MI5's counter-terrorism officer.

MPs have been targeted in a more direct way. Their opposition and concern in Cabinet forced Tony Blair, prime minister, to back down over moves to intercept members' calls. Such tapping had been banned for 40 years as a result of a ruling by Harold Wilson, the then Prime Minister. The tapping proposal came via a functionary, the Interception of Communications Commissioner, Sir Swinton Thomas. He is in touch with the security services, which would have had to be ready, willing and able to monitor MPs. Tony Blair said there had been inter-service recommendations.[4] MPs were worried that private information gained by tapping could have entered secret files on them.

Norman Baker, Liberal Democrat MP for Lewes, asked the Cabinet Office whether there had been a change of policy, not yet reported to the House of Commons. He wished to know how many MPs had been subjected to telephone tapping or other intrusive surveillance since 1966. His request was refused after both his initial letter and the internal review which followed. He was appealing to the Information Tribunal for release of the information.

Sir Swinton piled on further pressure with a report in February, 2007. He failed to see why MPs should be immune from interception.

Members of the intelligence community were astonished why this should be so.

Another issue was whether police should be allowed to bug MPs who had private meetings with those in whom they had legitimate interest. There were claims that the police now routinely bugged conversations between lawyers and their clients.[5]

Contingency plans are under way for an evacuation from Westminster to a substitute chamber in the countryside in the event of a crippling terrorist attack. MPs and Peers would sit at Bramshill, Hampshire, in the police staff college. Police, officials, catering staff and media would also be accommodated.[6]

Politicians are waking up to MI5. It has lost credibility following its intelligence failures over the suicide bombings in London and the raid in Forest Gate, east London, which led to police shooting an innocent suspect. A Conservative policy group on security proposed (26 July 2007) a dedicated homeland defence force to provide immediate assistance to Britain's civil authorities in the event of major terrorist incidents or other national emergencies, such as flooding. Strategies would be drawn up by a national security council. The group was led by Dame Pauline Neville-Jones, former head of the joint intelligence committee. The group links national security and diplomacy. The aim is that all Britain's military, internal security, diplomatic resources and actions abroad must work to enhance the security of the country and make the British people safer. Dame Pauline also became Shadow Security Minister.[7]

John Reid, when Home Secretary, evidently recognised that all was not well with the direction of anti-terrorist intelligence and action. In a fresh initiative introduced on 29 March 2007, the Prime Minister was to chair a security committee monthly and the Home Secretary decided to take a weekly strategic meeting. Whether that would make much difference would depend greatly on the quality of MI5 leadership and the extent to which the police were involved.

Those proposed changes were later to evolve into firmer control of anti-terrorism strategy with a 350-strong national security unit within the Home Office. Mr Reid succeeded in taking over the Cabinet Office's role in anti-terrorism strategy and winning a major victory over the Foreign Office. He assumed day-to-day co-ordination responsibility for MI6 (Secret Intelligence Service) with other agencies, although not ultimate oversight of it or of GCHQ. However, he had gained for the moment more power for joined-up spying. For Gordon Brown a bigger say in control of security was probably a worthwhile aim. The changes were part of a break-up of the old Home Office. Prisons, courts and probation now come under a new Ministry of Justice.

In a separate move, the Joint Committee on Human Rights, which consists of leading parliamentarians, had called for a new independent body to monitor the activities of MI5 and MI6. This was a blow to the Parliamentary body which was already charged with monitoring MI5 – the Intelligence and Security committee. The respectful, close relationship between the two was disclosed in correspondence which the Human Rights Committee members had published. The questions they put to Dame Eliza Manningham-Buller, head of MI5, demanded frank answers about issues which had caused outrage around the world. They asked for any information which the service might have about extraordinary renditions using UK airports. Such renditions are the transport of terrorist suspects to foreign jails where they may be tortured. The unspoken question was whether MI5 had used, perhaps unwittingly, information gained from torture.

Dame Eliza replied: 'I regret that I do not consider I can be of assistance to your committee in the areas outlined in your letter, all of which have been, or are, the subject of investigation by the ISC (Intelligence and Security Committee).'[8] Her brush-off reflects MI5's dislike of being put under searching scrutiny by those it regards as outsiders. As we shall see, the ISC has not gone overboard in its criticism of MI5. The Human Rights Committee members would ask questions of a kind which the ISC would not.

The acquiring of greater power without adequate scrutiny – MI5's achievement – is a feature of secret police in countries where democracy is not as prized as here. The Government has refused

35

a full inquiry into the suicide bomber attacks on London on 7 July 2005.

MI5 had earlier been involved in the miscarriages of justice in the scandalous cases of the Guildford Four and Birmingham Six, against a background of the IRA campaign.

Proclaiming their innocence, they had their convictions quashed by the Court of Appeal. MI5, which likes to be seen taking the lead in intelligence matters, remained discreetly in the background, while the police took the blame.

In 2007, continuing its push for power, MI5 took over the lead in tackling terrorism in Northern Ireland from the police. The police were in danger of being forced into second place nationally. MI5's success in getting extra money from the Treasury meant it was to have twice as many counter-terrorist officers as police, yet the police do more work in gathering evidence, initially within strict time limits. MI5's recruiting drive was planned to provide 3,200 staff by 2008 with more than 70 per cent dedicated to counter terrorism. According to *The Times*,[9] the Special Branch nationally and Scotland Yard's anti-terrorist squad then had only just over 1,000 officers devoted to countering terrorism. *The Times* had reported on 28 December 2005 that the police felt betrayed by the Government's failure to give them the money desperately needed in the fight to protect Britain from attack.[10]

MI5's drive for dominance began in the early 1990s when it took over from the Police Special Branch the lead in fighting mainland terrorism. The fault line between the best police traditions and MI5 is deep. MI5 are 'gentlemen' in old-style cricketing terms, the police 'players'. MI5 recruited government staff from the colonies when independence came, and their old attitudes, particularly towards race relations, were difficult to shake off. There have been changes in recruiting since, but the old sense of superiority expresses itself in disdain and overconfidence. Its sense of infallibility is not challenged enough because it operates in secret. Concern about keeping its mystique intact is one reason why MI5 fights so hard against proposals for a much-needed proper enquiry after the London bombings.

MI5's free-wheeling approach had led to other demands for an inquiry, this time by angry customs men. They wanted an investigation into allegations that MI5 organised the disappearance of a drugs baron, who had been given a 21-year sentence for a drug-smuggling operation. They were appalled by the way that a much decorated undercover agent died. *Timesonline* of 7 May 2005 said that the agent was one of a team who ambushed the alleged drugs baron's boat off the coast of Scotland in July 1996 and was crushed to death as he attempted to board the vessel while the alleged crime boss tried to destroy the three tonnes of cannabis said to be on board.[11]

The alleged drugs baron's version was that he was given a false identity by his handlers, then sent to Ireland to infiltrate Britain's biggest heroin gang. Nine weeks later he was found dead in a rundown benefits hostel in south London after, it is said, double-crossing MI5 and just hours before he was due to escape for a new life beyond the reach of British justice. The police said that a post-mortem examination showed he had died from natural causes.

Another MI5 case, this time involving an aged alleged spy forced the hand of Jack Straw, Home Secretary, who in September 1999 demanded tighter controls over the Service. MI5 decided not to prosecute, but still did not consult ministers. Straw told Stephen Lander, MI5's Director General, he wanted better oversight – by ministers – and an annual report on all operations against spies.[12]

MI5 has a history of using its powers to further its own agenda. Rogue agents are alleged to have been capable of conspiring subversively in ones or twos – or even more – to undermine the democratic process and intimidate those who offend them. MI5's rapid growth has to be seen against its controversial record of repeated unwarranted intrusion over many years. The *Guardian* discovered on 2 June 2003 that laws allowing British intelligence agents to bug and burgle were to be amended to allow bribery as well.[13]

The green light was to be given for further inroads into civil rights. John Reid said on 9 August 2006 that the 'challenge to all of us' meant 'we may have to modify some of our freedoms in the short term in order to prevent their misuse and abuse by those who oppose our fundamental values and would destroy our freedoms and values in the long term.'[14] The question is: how safe are those freedoms anyway, in our autocratic state?

Dame Eliza Manningham-Buller, MI5's then chief, raised the issue of a curb on civil liberties. She said in the Netherlands: 'There needs to be a debate on whether some erosion of what we all value may be necessary to improve the chances of our citizens not being blown apart as they go about their daily lives.'[15] She thus entered politics.

The intelligence agencies have been unrestrained. We will be examining evidence of the targeting of Princess Diana and, years before, of Compton Mackenzie, the author; of plotting against Harold Wilson, Prime Minister; of allegations by Colin Wallace, a Government information officer, that he was the victim of dirty tricks and there was sweeping condemnation in Parliament by Ken Livingstone, then London's Mayor, alleging MI5's misuse of power. We will show how the notorious Zinoviev letter incident, which undermined the Labour Party, was exposed through the initiative of Robin Cook, the Labour front-bencher. Princess Diana's former police bodyguard alleged that the intelligence agencies routinely taped her telephone conversations.

MI5's targets included union leaders during a miners' strike, and prominent members of CND. The disclosure came from Stella Rimingon, former head of MI5. In her memoirs, *Open Secret* (the *Guardian* 11 September 2001) she claimed a triumvirate in the National Union of Mineworkers 'had declared that they were using the strike to try to bring down the elected government and it was actively supported by the Communist Party'.[16] Dame Stella says the targeting of leading CND activists was justified. The anti-nuclear movement was 'entirely legitimate', but the Soviet Union found it of 'great interest' and encouraged the Communist Party of Great Britain to infiltrate it.

The first reports by MI5 on trade unions to be disclosed since the war were released in January 2001. They were into a two-week strike in 1970 by dockers over pay. It led to a state of emergency being declared and troops being put on stand-by. Reports on the strike, stamped 'top secret', by MI5's director general, Sir Martin Furnival-Jones, were sent to Edward Heath, the newly elected Prime Minister, every two or three days. They derived from bugging, agents' reports and phone tapping, giving details of private meetings involving Communist party officials and shop stewards. The editorial line of the *Morning Star* was 'the subject of much anxious consideration'.

The battle involving the unions reached a climax with the miners' strike of 1974 and the three-day week ending with Heath's election defeat. The tactics used by the miners hardened the resolve of Government to ensure that it would not be repeated (see Chapter 7). MI5's political subversion department was strengthened to meet left-wing militancy, and Dame Stella used the experience she had gained there when she led the service's operations against the miners' strike in 1984–85.

MI5's arm is far-reaching, and not always discriminating. The *Mail on Sunday* reported accusations that the Government was hoarding information about people who posed no threat to the country. It had emerged that MI5 held secret files on 272,000 individuals – 'a staggering one in 160 adults'. Another 53,000 files were held about organisations.[17]

The question is, what does it intend to do with them? We shall see in a later chapter.

Figures showing the extent to which information is gathered by intercepts or requested have shocked civil rights campaigners. Shami Chakrabarty, Liberty's director, said: 'There is a creeping contempt for our personal privacy.'[18]

During 2005–2006 requests for communications data totalled 439,054 according to Sir Swinton Thomas, the interception of communications commissioner. During the same period 3,972 errors were reported to his office – 2,712 by communications service providers and 1,260 by public authorities.

Smaller in number but more significant are the 66 errors and breaches reported in interception, an increase of 22 on the 2004 figure. Sir Swinton said the number was unacceptably high but in the previous 18 months intelligence and law enforcement agencies had been working under extreme pressure. None of the mistakes was deliberate and they were immediately nullified.

Nine agencies and organisations can lawfully intercept communications. Those bodies authorised to acquire communications data include 475 local authorities, the ambulance service and the fire service. Sir Swinton inspected and oversaw 795 organisations in all.[19]

Concern about MI5's poor judgement is of long standing. Criticism came from the formidable Lord Jenkins of Hillhead in the House of Lords on 9 December 1993. As Roy Jenkins he was Home Secretary and knew the security service well. Condemning MI5's political surveillance, he said:

That involves above all a fine judgement between what is subversion and what is legitimate dissent, which in my experience is unlikely to be found in those who live in the distorting and Alice through the Looking Glass world in which falsehood becomes truth, fact becomes fiction and fantasy becomes reality.

I would therefore pull MI5 totally out of its political surveillance role. I am almost equally doubtful about the associated internal political intelligence role.

Lord Jenkins thought that more supervision would be required, even if the service had a restricted role. He had experienced in the security service 'an inherent lack of frankness, an in-growing mono culture and a confidence destroying tendency to engage in the most devastating internal feuds'.[20]

Two days after the London bombings, Max Hastings, the defence specialist, wrote in the *Guardian* on 9 July 2005 that there were some outstanding brains in MI5 and MI6, and they were winning recruits. 'But the police and intelligence services also include lots of people who are simply not up to the challenge. They get it wrong with alarming frequency, which is why we cannot concede them unlimited powers.'[21]

This evidently persists. The *Mail on Sunday* disclosed on 14 January 2007 that confidential details sent to MI5 by thousands of individuals and businesses ended up with an American company specialising in supermarket mailshots. The security service's new e-mail early warning system was designed to reassure the public in the wake of July 7 bombings and a string of failed terror plots. 'People signing up to the alerts were asked to type their name and e-mail details into the MI5 website alongside an assurance their personal information would be protected by the Data Protection Act and the Security Services Act.' MI5 e-mailed them back: 'Thank you for your request to subscribe to the MI5/Home Office Threat Level Update e-mail list.' The *Mail* says that subscribers were led to believe their details were being kept in secure computer files at MI5's Thames House Headquarters in Whitehall.[22]

However, the *Mail on Sunday* revealed the service was not being run by MI5. Instead it had been paying What-Counts Inc, a US firm based in Seattle, to store the details and send terror alerts. This company specialised in sending advertising e-mails for retail firms. The *Mail on Sunday* said it had close ties with the US government and ran internet systems for the government-owned Voice of America broadcaster which had historic links to the CIA.

Whether a terror alert is of any value depends on the accuracy of intelligence. Less than 24 hours before the July 7 suicide bombings in London, Dame Eliza Manningham-Buller, then Director General of MI5, told a private meeting of Labour whips there was no imminent terrorist threat. This *Guardian* reporters found out from some of those present.[23]

The hybrid (SOCA) which was brought into being to fight organised crime under its ex-MI5 chief, Stephen Lander, was exposed as dysfunctional by Channel 4 News on 23 January 2007. The union which represents half SOCA's workforce claimed the agency had taken up only a fraction of the drugs cases referred to it. One SOCA investigator told the programme that the agency was paralysed by bureaucracy. Channel 4 News reported that some SOCA officers were so disillusioned that they had already left the agency. There was renewed concern about staff morale with the disclosure in *Computing* (26 July 2007) that eight staff in the electronics crime department had left SOCA in the previous four months amid concerns over the operation of the unit.

Timesonline noted on 17 February 2007 an admission by Lander that morale was mixed. But there had been record seizures of cocaine at home and abroad, although it was not clear by whom. Nearly £8 million worth of fake cheques and postal orders were seized in Nigeria among items intended for mass marketing fraud. SOCA worked with local law enforcers. After sifting through 56,000 people recorded on the National Criminal Intelligence Service database SOCA was targeting 2,000 who were considered to be crucial. It was not clear who would be bringing to justice the remaining 54,000. Presumably they would not have been on the database if they were not originally of interest to law enforcers, although there were some duplications.[24]

The Agency has more of MI5 about it than traditional police squads. 'This organisation needs to be knowledge before action,' Sir Stephen Lander said. He was speaking at the Centre for Crime and Justice Studies at King's College, London, at a meeting sponsored by *The Times*.[25] SOCA's first annual report on 18 May 2007 reads more like publicity than the sober, detached self-examination of other official bodies without such an apparent need to justify themselves. Eulogies to SOCA from admirers are quoted on at least five pages of its annual report. However, crucial numerical targets set for SOCA were for the recovery of UK criminal assets, and in 2006/07 it achieved none. It could claim that the cases were a legacy from the National Crime Squad, but SOCA cuts across other people's work all the time. The report admits: 'There are no crimes where SOCA has a monopoly of response.' That being so, its success must depend at least partly on others, and credit for it cannot be claimed by SOCA alone.[26]

Bill Hughes, SOCA's director general, is quoted as saying that creation of the agency had been complicated. But the first annual staff turnover of 3.9 per cent was good for the public service, and morale was high.[27]

It is time to look at MI5 more closely, to see in the next chapter if it is capable of living up to the demands on it and high expectations the State has of it.

4

Spying on Princess Diana, MPs and Journalists

My trouble with MI5 began when an ex-officer I met let it be known that I had been under scrutiny for years. I later obtained corroborative evidence that my telephone was tapped.

Afterwards I set out to explore why I had been targeted and to try and get an idea of the acute pressure evidently put on people who had nothing to do with terrorism and were innocent of subversion. The cost of this scrutiny must have been considerable, given the resources which are always claimed to be necessary for surveillance, and it must have been a distraction from the effort that should have been put into preventing terrorist murders.

As a non-committed journalist I had first been offered unique access to MI5 in 1966. My personal interest continued after formal meetings with its officers had ended. MI5 was anxious about what I would write. It was not my intention to produce anything at that time (the 1980s and 1990s). I knew MI5 was bent on gaining more power and was not properly accountable. I needed to know what that would lead to. Today I do, from observation and private contacts, and MI5 has in any case become a subject of acute public interest. The disclosure by an ex-officer that MI5 was targeting me showed its interest went far beyond the meetings I agreed to, and that it was prepared to invade my privacy for its own active purposes. MI5 therefore legitimised my own investigation of it in return.

One of my tasks in 1967 for *The Times* was to lead six journalists in a news team investigation on three continents into Maoists and black people's struggles in Africa, America and Britain. The guarded steers I was given by MI5 were useful, not least about the movements of the Black Power leader Stokely Carmichael, as he spread his message abroad. A Maoist propagandist whom the team exposed had taken tea with Chou-en-lai in Beijing before coming to Britain. It was not my role to feed MI5 men with information, although what they knew on occasions confirmed what we had learnt already. As always, I accepted nothing on trust. It was checked out.[1]

It was, however, impossible for me not to be of use eventually, since the news team's findings were published and available. It was in MI5's interest that I should know where to look. This was particularly useful in finding out about links between the Maoist headquarters in Brussels and activists in this country, which we then uncovered for ourselves.

After the resulting series appeared in *The Times*, two MI5 men arranged a meeting at the Charing Cross Hotel, where they told me that, in one important respect, the news team had found out more than MI5 had. Before we left, the MI5 men took the cushions out from every chair and checked that nothing had been left, although none of us had produced any papers.

My discovery that MI5's performance was in one respect inferior to ours became significant later when I was assessing the agency's abilities in the light of the terrorist attack on London. It had been a surprise to hear that MI5 was not better than it was, given the surveillance at which it was supposed to excel, as well as telephone tapping, letter opening and the monitoring power of GCHQ. I knew how MI5 opened the mail because it happened to a letter of mine which had been sent to a revolutionary, with a cheque in it, to pay for information. He was trying to be a journalist. MI5's question about it was not direct and specific but oblique and non-committal, and my reply was even more so.

The revolutionary I had got to know had asked me what he had to do to be a journalist. 'Sell information,' I said. 'What sort?' he asked. 'Have you got any guns?' I said. 'You're trying to get me to sell my friends down the river,' he replied. 'Well, you asked me what stories a journalist might write about and I told you.' As I had another informant in Michael 'X''s group, to which the revolutionary belonged, I found out later that my contact had told a meeting of my request. I concluded by double-checking that they had no guns.

MI5 sometimes wished to plant information, but I never used any of that kind. I was told a story about Vanessa Redgrave, which was in effect a smear. I did not see why an actress of her quality should be denigrated by spies, and ignored the information. Sometimes my contacts were useful for double-checking. When Michael 'X' claimed that one of his group was 'my Vietnamese friend', I asked about it and was shown a photograph from a source which established he wasn't Vietnamese. The Vietnam war was raging at the time. It was just one of Michael's sinister little tales and I had never really believed it anyway.

While I was no informer, I thought it in the public interest to warn generally of a potential conflict between police and the black community. My instincts were aroused by a clash I reported between police and a small number of young black people in Notting Hill, the first of its kind. I had a meeting arranged anyway with Sir Arthur Peterson, then Permanent Under-Secretary at the Home Office, and told him of my concerns. Nobody seemed to do anything about the approaching danger. The people from MI5 I spoke to did not express any interest. Eventually I met someone from the Prime Minister's office who seemed more prepared to listen. Even when I went to stay with a black family with young sons in Brixton and wrote about anger in the community it had only one effect – the wrong effect – on the MI5 man I met. He had read what I had written: I had gone behind what black people called 'the front line'. He thought I was inciting trouble by using the phrase 'the front line'.

It was a useful insight. MI5 sees the world as it wishes it to be, based on preconceptions, and not always as it actually is, from other people's viewpoints. There was also a failure to understand that my writing in *The Times* did not follow a particular line, but treated each news item on its merits. MI5 obviously expected a line to be followed, which implied it did not expect an open-minded approach. At worst, its own attitudes were prejudiced: they were pre-judged. This was later to lead to misjudgements on a grand scale, with the failure to tackle Islamist hate merchants in Britain in the 1990s and intelligence failures over the London bombings and the fiasco at Forest Gate, east London. Sometimes I marvel at the extreme certainty with which some talking heads, formerly associated with intelligence, express themselves when broadcasting. They assert things boldly off the tops of their heads which a moderately good journalist would first need to check out and then double check with several sources. There are, of course, many experts whose knowledge and balance are highly professional.

The contacts I met were, with a very few exceptions, unimpressive, perhaps because at heart they were bureaucrats. Most would not have been good enough for employment on a local paper. I speak as someone who was involved at one time in the selection of staff for *The Times*. The contacts I met were not streetwise, and said and did the obvious. They lacked perception and an ability to see implications. Original ideas were usually alien to them, and were treated with suspicion. They tended to be stuck in the last crisis rather than foreseeing the next one. There is still some nostalgia for the old days. They knew where they were in the Cold War and Northern Ireland. Nevertheless, the quality of their technical staff at bugging and clandestine filming is impressive. I found their discernment and judgement to be weak, however.

Their complacency and overconfidence sprang from the absence of challenge. Protected in their secret world, they never faced criticism of the kind that journalists do with letters to the editor or that police experience on a regular basis when giving evidence in court. When having a clandestine lunch, it was more important not to pick up a piece of lettuce with your fingers than to raise serious questions. Watching individuals was MI5's work, and seeing who was connected with whom. MI5 cannot handle criticism, preferring to shroud itself in mystique, and thinking, rather, that it deserves deference. It prefers spin doctoring to frankness.

Officers never really understood the media, thinking of them as a sort of wayward second cousin, the sort who in the good old days would have been sent as a remittance man to the colonies – dangerous, non-conformist and to be kept in their place.

Partly by accident, I had found myself, as a journalist, privy to attempts to spy on and manipulate the media and use journalists to do so. My formal contact with MI5 ended when, over lunch, I was asked to spy for it. I immediately refused.

Jon Snow, presenter of Channel 4 News, was also invited by the intelligence services in 1976 to work for them, but he too refused,[2] It later became known that Tim Jones, one of my colleagues, was approached by MI5 in 1975, and he, too, refused to co-operate with them. The *Independent* carried the story on 29 September 1987 under the headline 'MI5 tried to recruit spy at *Times*'. Tim met an MI5 man for lunch at Simpsons in the Strand.

I did not come into the open myself at that point because I would have destroyed any chance of finding out more. Although my formal relationship with MI5 had ended, my informal observations of the intelligence world had not. As time went on, I was to meet other contacts. I was convinced that the real story was yet to come and I was still in a good position as a journalist to get it.

My experience of getting close to people I have investigated long term taught me that the greatest chance of success came if I didn't have to write anything while I was embedded with them. It worked when finding out about conspiracies by black activists and Maoists – one of my contacts, Michael 'X', was later hanged for murder. But when I did write something about a London gangster an associate got on the phone to me and said: 'I'm coming round to deal with you physically.'

I had no doubt that secret files were also being kept on other journalists, particularly if they were covering 'sensitive' subjects or were possible candidates for spying. David Leigh, a former colleague on *The Times*, wrote in the *British Journalism Review*: 'British journalists – and British journals – are being manipulated by the secret intelligence agencies and I think we ought to try and put a stop to it.'[3] The article was re-printed in the *Guardian* of 12 June 2000. Leigh said that one form of the manipulation was an attempt to recruit journalists to spy on other people or to go themselves under journalistic 'cover'.

The evidence I had unearthed showed Leigh to be right. I learnt that the British media were being looked at in depth. I had discovered when regularly lecturing to police that the questions they asked revealed more about their attitudes than my answers did about mine. The same was true when a clandestine contact asked me about the way newspapers worked. I gave a basic run-down, such as I might give to a general audience, and revealed nothing confidential. All except one of the follow-up questions were elementary, and of a kind that might be asked by an intelligent Woman's Institute audience. The exception was about a colleague, Bernard Levin, then a swingeing columnist on *The Times*. His work was evidently under scrutiny as a major dissident about almost everything, except his beloved Wagner. I did not mention anything that an idiot could not have picked up already from Bernard's writing. I was asked if he had a licence to write anything he liked. I replied truthfully that I did not know, except the obvious – that the editor was ultimately responsible for everything in the paper. I guessed, but did not say, that if Bernard thought himself censored he would take his business elsewhere. When a memo came round to journalists limiting the number of words that could be used in a sentence, Bernard's next sentence was, as I recall, 95 words long. I thought to myself that nothing would deter Bernard and he could look after himself and would continue to write as he always had. Had I told him my story, he might sensibly have blown it in his column.

The outcome of the then secret study was revealed in *The Times* on 22 February 2005. Alan Hamilton wrote what had previously been forecast: '*The Times* would merge with the *Financial Times*, the *Daily Mail* with the *Daily Express*, Rupert Murdoch would buy the London *Evening News* and *The People* would close within years.'[4]

None of it happened. Harold Wilson had asked Lord Rothschild to make an assessment of the newspaper industry, then hit by overmanning and soaring newsprint prices. *The Times* did not mention the clandestine connection, presumably because it was not revealed. It becomes clearer from reading *Spycatcher*, written by Peter Wright, an ex-agent.[5] He says that in 1958 he was introduced to a man who did more than most to secure the modernisation of MI5, Victor Rothschild. He worked inside MI5 during the war and won the George Medal for opening bombs. Rothschild maintained close friendships with many of the senior officers.

My hunch that something was up began to come true. Peter Wright in *Spycatcher*, in his disclosure of the plotting against Harold Wilson, confirmed that MI5 was seeking power to impose its view of the world. Later, MI5 began to make inroads into the police by taking the lead against terrorism and elbowing its way into fighting serious crime. The end of the Cold War had taken away some of its work and it seized the chance to gain influence elsewhere.

It was also becoming apparent that, historically and now, MI5 was using its muscle against those it did not see as conforming to its narrow right-wing outlook. Its secret influence included political vetting at the BBC via the personnel department, which was eventually exposed in the *Observer* in 1985.[6] Attempts were made by MI5 to block the career of Anna Ford, the talented television journalist and newsreader, because she was alleged to have a boyfriend who was a former member of the Communist Party. MI5's vetting is now regarded as having been ruthless, narrowly dogmatic, prosaic and unimaginative.

One of those whom MI5 attempted to blacklist was Roland Joffé. Mark Hollingsworth and Richard Norton-Taylor say in *Blacklist* he was 'probably Britain's most distinguished film and television director'. He won an Academy Award nomination and top prize at the 1986 Cannes Film Festival. His appointment by the BBC as director of a new play, *The Spongers*, was confirmed only after a huge internal row. It won the prestigious *Prix Italia* award.[7]

The author, Sir Compton Mackenzie, was hounded by MI5 for years after revealing embarrassing secrets about the security and intelligence services, according to documents released at the national archives.[8]

New light has been thrown on the Zinoviev letter, a scandal lingering from the 1920s. The letter, a forgery, purported to come from the president of Comintern to the central committee of the Communist Party of Great Britain, urging it to agitate the proletariat for class war. Four days after the letter appeared in the *Daily Mail*, the Labour Party lost the general election to the Conservatives. A report by the Foreign Office after new research shows that two intelligence officers were among those involved in leaking the letter to the *Daily Mail* and Conservative Central Office. However, the research found no organised plot against Labour by intelligence organisations.

The net has been spread far and wide. Princess Diana's former police bodyguard alleged that the intelligence agencies routinely taped her telephone conversations at the time she made an intimate call to an admirer in 1989. The story was carried in *The Sunday Times* on 25 August 2002. Inspector Ken Wharfe, who was her senior police protection officer at the time, says that Diana

> was aware that the intelligence agencies monitored the daily lives of the royal family.
>
> Royalty protection department officers were categorically not involved in this surveillance. For my part, I simply accepted that any such steps would be a necessary part of her security, and warned the princess to be aware, and went about my business.
>
> I did not know until much later that they routinely taped the princess's telephone conversations.[9]

Mr Wharfe assumed that the Princess and other members of the royal family were under regular surveillance because of heightened

IRA activity.[10] He told the inquest into her death of his belief that the telephone conversation with her friend, James Gilbey, known as the Squidgygate tapes, may have been recorded by GCHQ, the government's secret communication agency. A transcript was published in a national newspaper in 1992.

John Major, then prime minister, issued a statement denying that the security services had recorded the call.

'Mr Wharfe, like others before him, was unable to explain how the conversation was then picked up by two amateur radio operators living in Oxfordshire,' *The Times* said. His interpretation, although lacking factual backing, comes from someone more knowledgeable than most about security.

To provide reassurance, the Queen's rooms were regularly checked for bugging devices, the inquest heard.[11] The sweeps were carried out by the security services, according to Lord Fellowes, the Queen's private secretary in the 1990s and Diana's brother-in-law. He said that the then Home Secretary had prevented a full security service investigation of what happened because of concerns that the press would misrepresent the move.

Sir Richard Dearlove, former head of M16, told the inquest (then continuing) into the deaths of Diana and Dodi Fayed that any eavesdropping, surveillance or bugging of Diana would have been 'outside of the function of the service'. Whether significantly or not, he was not reported as saying 'outside of the function of the services'.[12]

There was a bungled spy operation against the Pakistan High Commission, and Clare Short MP claims that the UK bugged Kofi Annan, the UN Secretary General. The revelations about the runaway intelligence services begin to sound similar. A former MI5 agent, Annie Machon, describes in her book *Spies, Lies & Whistleblowers* (Book Guild) illegal intelligence operations, cover-ups to ministers and MI6 funding of al-Qaeda operations.[13]

Her inside knowledge makes more plausible an extraordinary attack by Ken Livingstone in the House of Commons on 10 January 1996. He said: 'The existence of MI5 is a threat to democracy in this country, and has been terribly damaging, fatal in some cases, to those who have been on the receiving end of it.' MI5 should be broken up, he said. Any worthwhile bits should be given to the police to operate as usefully as they could within the law.

Livingstone said MI5 believed that seven members of Harold Wilson's government and three other Labour Members of Parliament were either spies or, at the very least, security risks. Only one of the ten turned out eventually to be guilty. All the others on MI5's list were completely innocent. 'But that did not stop MI5, in particular Peter Wright, hounding Bernard Floud, who had been devastated by the death of his wife. MI5 pursued him until he finally committed suicide in a moment of despair.'[14]

Livingstone's statement can be compared with disclosures in Annie Machon's book about the journalist, Victoria Brittain, who worked for the *Guardian*. She 'posed no threat to security but was in essence persecuted by MI5 for over a year'. As a normal part of her job Brittain had met a Cuban who, unknown to her, was in reality an intelligence officer working under diplomatic cover. This brought her to the notice of MI5. It then became interested in an innocent Libyan angle.

Before Joan Ruddock, chairperson of CND, became an MP, she was targeted.

Between 1981 and 1986 I was frequently subjected, as a direct consequence of my involvement in CND, to frightening and intimidating behaviour. I shall never know whether those events related to MI5, but I feel certain that my privacy – and that of my family – was systematically invaded, and my character impugned with absolutely no justification.[15]

She said that according to Cathy Massiter, a former MI5 officer, 'my file grew and grew'.

It is against this background that I will give my own experience of attempted hounding and intrusion. I knew too much, particularly about attempts to penetrate the media and needed to be deterred. I was aware of a failed attempt to enrol someone running a BBC programme which would have allowed its slant and content to be influenced. Today, with MI5 men controlling operations in SOCA, in parliamentary security and in an alternative police force up and down the land there is more opportunity for its views to prevail than ever before. I was in the way.

Two men associated with the security world began showing a close interest in me in the 1990s. A third man, a retired neighbour, had worked in the same top secret area as one of the other two. He was evidently troubled by what he was now doing. He told me he was taking the numbers of all the cars belonging to people who called at my house. He went to a book to look up further details, he said. He told me he had also noted people coming to my house. He was, it seemed, carrying out observation dutifully but had a divided loyalty. He was a bachelor pensioner and friend, and he has since died. We always invited him to share our Christmas dinner. After he revealed his snooping, I fished out from under the Christmas tree a present for him – a cheap pair of binoculars so that he could see the car numbers more easily.

The surveillance, worthy of the *Stasi*, appeared to me, however, to be ludicrous and time-wasting. A car with two men in it parked regularly to the side of my property were said not to be potential burglars but to be on surveillance duty when I inquired through sources. Yet they were unlike any policeman I had come across in my job doing surveillance. Unless police wish to be noted, perhaps as a deterrent, they vary their movements and are better disguised.

A similar thought occurred to me when a large black saloon car, unmarked and uninvited, drove suddenly into the gravel forecourt of my house. A slightly nervous young woman rang the doorbell and asked if she and her male colleague could carry out surveillance. I asked if they would like some tea. As I handed it to them I inquired if they would mind if I carried on with some gardening.

While they read newspapers in the car outside my window, I fetched weed-killer and slowly and methodically sprayed it on the gravel all round them. Eventually they had enough – I was observing them more closely than they were observing me or anyone else. The man in the passenger seat pulled his baseball hat down over his eyes in a gesture of resignation and they drove off without a word.

The next intrusion aroused suspicions that my telephone was being tapped. I can corroborate fully the statement (below) by the source I was speaking to, who wishes to remain anonymous. We agreed to try and find out more. The results were bizarre, but apparently not so in the surreal world of intelligence, My source states:

After finishing a conversation I put the receiver down. Immediately the phone rang and a strange voice repeated to me the last few words said by P.E.

To test whether there was intrusion on the telephone, we decided to use words which might provoke a third-party reaction. When I said 'coup d'état' the line immediately went dead.

By now our suspicions had increased, and we tried to provoke 'the hidden voice'. To see what further reaction there could be from provocation, P.E. decided to make a telephone call to me in which he would insult two senior people with security connections. He reasoned that they would feel insulted only if they got to hear what he said. They could not feel insulted if the conversation remained private. P.E. likened them to dogs in the rudest repeatable way.

P.E. rang me to say that a bag of excrement had been left on the grass verge outside his property. While this was an interesting sequence, we felt that it might just have been a coincidence and needed to be tested further. After an interval, P.E. said to me on the telephone that in its bullying, intimidation and blackmail MI5 was worse than the Kray twins. The sequence was a bag of excrement in my drive. Afterwards, we thought that two such events in response to deliberately provocative telephone calls were stretching coincidences too far. There was to us a cause and an effect. We felt there was corroborative evidence to give some support to our suspicions of telephone tapping.

We concluded that the excrement came from a dog or dogs. P.E. has asked himself since who would have had enough dogs in one place to produce as much excrement in so quick a response.

It dawned on us that, if the telephone were being tapped and we were being listened to, we could turn the tables and use the intrusion to our own advantage.

P.E. therefore began a campaign of ridicule and black propaganda over the telephone to attack anyone apparently listening in to us. To sabotage the usefulness of any telephone tapping, P.E. included falsehoods in the conversations and said he was doing so.

I have asked myself why ordure from dogs was dumped when it obviously gave the game away, However, MI5 had already implied that my telephone was been tapped when I learnt I was subject to deep investigation, and this was presumably continuing. Both men I was targeting were self-important and one was decidedly vain. That meant they were easy to provoke. There could also have been a desire to crush me for daring to retaliate. MI5 had a record of successful hounding, as we have seen. The priority was evidently attempted intimidation of me. I needed to be deterred. I knew MI5 thought it was untouchable – and a failure to hold an inquiry into the London bombings showed that to be true.

If the telephone were being tapped, there might be a wider audience, so I decided to retaliate, inspired by Sefton Delmer, the *Daily Express* journalist who had turned his hand to black propaganda during the 1939–45 war, demoralising the Germans. If the telephone were tapped, the transcript would not be circulated only to a single person. This meant that anything I said would reverberate around the Secret State.

In the midst of my vigorous campaign, the two suspects I targeted went out of contact and I haven't seen them since. Their cover was evidently blown.

Another man who also made a point of getting to know me told me, with a moment's hesitation when asked, that he had worked with the Home Office against terrorism. He said I was not going to be subjected to any more pressure. It sounded to me like a patronising peace offering which I resolved not to accept. He associated with two evident companions whose close attention was unwelcome.

In a telephone conversation with my anonymous collaborator, I recalled Gilbert and Sullivan's *Mikado* ('Three little maids from school') but changed the words of Yum-Yum, Peep-Bo and Pitti-Sing.

Three little spies at work are we,
Daft as only a spook can be,
Misreading all that we can see.

Yum-Yum: We know full well we are second to none.
Peep Bo: Nobody's safe when we are done.
Pitti-Sing: Our grimy work has just begun.
Yum-Yum, Peep-Bo and Pitti-Sing (dancing)

Three little spies at work.
Three little spies who all too wary
Each thinks she's a luminary,
Bullying people, so contrary.

Three little spies at work.

Stella Rimington, first woman director of MI5, admitted in a lengthy interview in *Guardian Weekend* that 'from the position of 2001' files were opened on people who were not actively threatening the State. In the past 'some of our predecessors may have been a bit over-enthusiastic'.[16]

They still are, and I am fascinated by their techniques. My MI5 contact, who was involved in following a quarry when I bumped into him, thus illustrated how straightforward pursuit worked. The police I got to know over the years also gave me insight into surveillance techniques. Observers glance at their wristwatches – a give-away – to see the time when something is worth noting. It may have to be quoted in court. Some spies are quaint. Retired gentlemen of the old school and dressed smartly in tweeds would fit better into the Cotswolds than London.

When I visited a police headquarters outside London for a special news feature a senior officer went out of his way to introduce me to a nondescript man especially there from the Ministry of Defence (MI5's cover in those days), all by himself, drinking out of a cup. He was embarrassed and didn't want to look at me. The first hijacked aircraft to be diverted to Stansted was at first thought by police to be an exercise by MI5, a senior Scotland Yard officer told me. I also learnt from one retired MI5 man his vehement dislike of the police.

My regular contact with officers arranged by MI5 did not lead to anything factually reportable and what I discovered of interest came from elsewhere. I learnt nothing officially from my meetings about intimidation techniques. They may allow targeted individuals to know they are being watched and followed, particularly if they need to be pressurised. Getting close to someone – invading their space – is intended to disconcert. Crowding someone, if two officers are involved, can be done by following the target into a confined space, say a public lavatory. Passing guarded remarks in a restaurant relevant to a targeted person so that they can be overheard is part of the game. Or if the person is known to hold something dear, criticism of it has two aims – firstly to show how much is known about him or her and secondly to rubbish it.

The mobile phone is an aid to a surveillance operation. Text messages to a watching agent can help with co-ordination without being too obtrusive.

An old trick is to put a coin or two, say a 10p piece, outside someone's front door. It certainly will not deter the robust, but may make the susceptible pause, especially if done repeatedly. Windows are sometimes more useful than they seem. Sitting in a train may allow a reflection to reveal the passenger in the seat behind. Shop windows can also be useful, depending on the light and what is behind them, as a means of seeing what is going on to the rear of you without drawing attention to yourself.

At my first meeting with an MI5 officer in the Waldorf Hotel, London, a man appeared carrying a huge old-fashioned tape-recorder and made a point of slowly walking close to the table where we were sitting. 'One of yours?' I asked the MI5 man who couldn't disguise his annoyance. I had built up very helpful relationships in the law and order field and, whether or not it was intended, the recorder acted as a warning.

I had to give a talk on my experiences as a journalist to an organisation which Sir Stephen Lander, the former MI5 chief, by apparent coincidence, wished to join on that very evening. He had become chairman of SOCA (Serious Organised Crime Agency). A month before my talk I was invited to a small dinner party with him. He couldn't come to the talk because he was up for election to the organisation that evening, and the rules did not allow it. He sent a message saying how sorry he was to miss the talk. Another MI5 man also sent at the same time a message to me via a third party I knew, saying how he had enjoyed the cosy evenings in my house (years ago before he joined the Security Service). I had not heard from him since and have heard nothing since the meeting. A third, retired member of MI5, also telephoned me. It was he who had had first introduced me to MI5. We had a desultory conversation. Then he asked casually: 'Are you giving any talks these days?' Yes, I said, on the whereabouts of the bones of our local saint, and during the next 20 minutes took him back to the fourth century AD. They need not have worried that I was going to say anything nasty about MI5. My talk was on a different subject.

What I had learnt about the use of pressure on individuals put the death of Dr David Kelly, the former senior UN weapons inspector, in a new light. The Hutton inquiry concluded he took his own life. Dr Kelly was found dead on 18 July 2003 after it emerged he was the possible source of a BBC story which embarrassed the Government over its claims of weapons of mass destruction in Iraq. Many now think that Dr Kelly's death was suspicious, and some believe that he was murdered. It may be seen in the context of evidence about other clandestine pressure on people, assembled for this book. Bernard Floud, a former communist who later became a Labour MP, committed suicide. Ken Livingstone told the Commons Floud had been hounded by MI5. Politicians, from Harold Wilson down, were targeted. So was Compton Mackenzie, the author. Pressure was evidently put on Denis Donaldson, a murdered Sinn Fein man who worked as a double agent for British intelligence and the Special Branch. He had said he was recruited as a spy after compromising himself at a vulnerable time in his life. The journalist, Victoria Brittain, was harassed, as we have seen. Joan Ruddock received unwelcome attention.

We know Dr Kelly was under pressure anyway. But there appears to have been something more. He is reported to have sent an e-mail message to a journalist on the morning he went missing, saying there were 'many dark actors playing games'. Like others who might be threatened, he knew too much.

My approach to M15 was guarded. The comment of one of my clandestine contacts had registered with me. He said that it would be surprising if I were the only person on *The Times* that MI5 was in touch with. I did not wish to endanger the mission I had set myself by being compromised by someone I did not know to be a friend of MI5. At least one senior person was; and another, also in authority, made it plain that he was aware of my interest in the subject. They left me alone. Both are dead.

But when the time was ripe for me to make a comment publicly, using the 40 years' knowledge and experience I had gained of MI5, I chose to offer a letter to the editor of *The Times*, which was published as follows:

Sir, Dame Eliza Manningham-Buller's concern about the terrorist threat should be regarded as an urgent call for more police to tackle it, rather than a need for further growth in the power and strength of MI5.

The police are answerable to the public and MI5 is not. We need to know what value for money would result from more resources for MI5. But we cannot know because MI5 will not tell us. The quality of police investigation in recent months has been obvious, along with the enormous effort needed to go through sources of evidence. The police seek to be transparent, as their press briefings show.

There were no speeches, however, by Eliza Manningham-Buller apologising publicly for intelligence failures by MI5 before the London bombings and the Forest Gate fiasco in East London. If MI5 tried effectively to get at Islamist hate merchants in the 1990s and some of them later, it has not been very obvious. The Government has protected MI5 from an inquiry into the London bombings, although urgently requested by many.

In January this year you ran a report that stated: 'MI5 will soon employ twice as many counter-terrorist officers as the police, after an injection of extra money from the Treasury last month.'

The Government should get more value for money for our better protection.

This means spending it on the police.

The letter was published on 13 November 2006. A month later, on 14 December, Dame Eliza, MI5's chief, announced her resignation. She had been only four years in the job.

5

Judges Under Attack

Draconian laws introduced to stop the bombers produced unprecedented anger by ministers over their interpretation by judges. The courts were being challenged in their role as an independent bastion of liberty.

John Reid, Home Secretary, and Tony Blair, Prime Minister, attacked judges for the way they were handling the law on control orders, intended to contain suspects. Tony Blair's outburst came in response to a question about the absconding of two terrorist suspects subject to control orders and under virtual house arrest. He blamed the courts and opposition MPs for so weakening the Government's anti-terrorism measures that the control order regime was left fallible.

He said at his monthly news conference on 17 October 2006: 'We, of course, wanted far tougher laws against terrorism. We were prevented by opposition in parliament and then by the courts in ensuring that was done.

'I wanted to make sure that the original anti-terrorist legislation was maintained in full. Control orders were never going to be as effective as detention.'

For the Government the absconding was a huge embarrassment. The orders are issued by the Home Secretary to control the movements and actions of those deemed to need it.

John Reid had earlier attacked a ruling by the three most senior judges that meant 'six Iraqi terror suspects', all asylum seekers, would receive less severe treatment under their control orders.

Curfews would be reduced. He intended to challenge in the House of Lords the ruling made by an Appeal Court panel led by Lord Phillips, the Lord Chief Justice. They found 'compelling' a ruling by Mr Justice Sullivan that control orders making the suspects stay 18 hours a day indoors amounted to imprisonment by other means. They were rather like prisoners in a cell. The judges said this was against Article 5 of the Human Rights Convention, which prevents indefinite detention without trial. The control orders were quashed.

Mr Reid re-imposed the orders, adjusting them to ensure their rights to liberty. That meant being kept 14 hours a day inside instead of 18 and no vetting of people they wished to meet. However, they would be prevented from meeting those regarded by the Home Office as dangerous.

The new orders, said Mr Reid, were not as stringent as the security services believed were necessary – the influence of MI5 on law enforcement and restrictions is thus revealed. He intended to appeal to the House of Lords, 'not least because I'm concerned about its effects on public safety. We are at a sustained high level of threat from a terrorist attack. Control orders form an essential part of our fight against terrorism.'[1] However, the Law Lords said that 18-hour curfews breached the human right to liberty. They found the curfews on 'six Iraqis' to be too harsh, and three out of five ruled the Home Secretary should be able to impose only shorter ones. But the overall system was legal. (*Independent.co.uk*, 1 November 2007.)[2]

The conflict came to a head on 24 May 2007 after another three terrorist suspects absconded while under control orders. John Reid said new proposals would be brought forward within the next few weeks. He blamed political opponents and judges for stopping the use of tougher measures. 'I hope when we bring forward new proposals in the next weeks that we shall have a little less party politics and a little more support for national security.'[3]

The most far-reaching decision in the series came when high court judges ruled that two Libyan terror suspects could not be sent home to Colonel Gadafy's realm because of a risk of torture and show trial. The ruling, by the Special Immigration Appeals Commission, undermined Tony Blair's policy of obtaining assurances from regimes that they would not torture foreign terror suspects returned to them. The decision affected eight more terror suspects detained in Long Lartin maximum security prison. (*Guardian*, 28 April 2007.)

The two men, known only as DD and AS, were to be released on bail with 13 strict conditions, including a 12-hour curfew and no access to the internet or to mobile phones. John Reid, Home Secretary, was intending to appeal against the ruling. The judges said the agreement had been signed in good faith by Libya. But Mr Justice Ouseley, chairman of the Special Immigration Appeals Commission, said that if the two men were returned to Libya there was a real, but not probable, risk the European Convention would be breached. Assurances of a fair trial could not be taken at face value. The ruling regime might not be able to resist the temptation to interrogate the men. (*Timesonline*, 28 April 2007.)

The Court of Appeal blocked the return of the two terrorist suspects, AS and DD. Deportation cases against another ten Libyan suspects were dropped by the Home Office after legal advice that it would lose them, Tony Blair's policies on repatriation were thus badly damaged. (*Timesonline*, 10 April 2008.)

Control Orders were created in March 2005 after the Law Lords held that the detention of twelve foreigners in Belmarsh high security prison for more than three years without charge was illegal. They had been arrested in the wake of the 9/11 attacks in the United States. The orders were issued by the Home Secretary against suspected terrorists whom the Government was unable to prosecute through lack of evidence or because the evidence would jeopardise another investigation. The orders were made to control their movements and actions, and could, for example, prevent them from leaving their home, contacting particular people or places or using the internet. Cutting off their phones, tagging them and subjecting them to unannounced visits by MI5 kept them under scrutiny. If nevertheless they broke the conditions of the order it was a criminal offence, but the order itself did not carry with it a criminal charge.

The battleground of litigation brought the courts into conflict with the Government's tough proposals. The orders replaced emergency laws introduced following the 9/11 outrages which empowered the Government to imprison a number of foreign terror suspects without charge or trial. The Human Rights Act forbade them being sent to countries where there was a risk of them being tortured or ill-treated in other ways.

The inside story of the reaction of the courts to enforcement of the laws against terrorism was provided by the Lord Chief Justice, Lord Phillips of Worth Matravers, in the annual lecture to the Singapore Academy of Law on 29 August 2006.[4]

Lord Phillips described a House of Lords judgement in the continuing saga to have been 'one of the most dramatic to have been given in my time in the law'. The Lords hearing derived from controversial measures under anti-terrorism legislation. The 2001 Act allowed the Home Secretary to issue a certificate relating to an alien if he reasonably believed that the person's presence in the United Kingdom was a risk to national security and suspected the person was a terrorist. Under section 23 of the Act the alien was subject to detention and deportation. If the risk of torture, for example, made it impossible to deport him, then he could be detained indefinitely in the UK without trial, pending ultimate deportation.

The Secretary of State issued certificates in relation to a number of aliens that he was unable to deport, and they were detained in Belmarsh Prison. They exercised their right to appeal.

Exceptionally, nine Law Lords sat to hear it. The outcome was 'a severe blow to the Government's anti-terrorism strategy,' Lord Phillips said. The House of Lords declared that section 23 of the 2001 Act was incompatible with the Human Rights Convention.

The Government, defeated, introduced new legislation – the Prevention of Terrorism Act 2005 – which brought in control orders.

On one of the issues facing the court Lord Hoffmann, 'in a lone and Churchillian dissent', said: 'Terrorist violence, serious as it is, does not threaten our institutions of government or our existence as a civil community.' He added: 'The real threat to the life of the nation, in the sense of a people living in accordance with its traditional laws and political values, comes not from terrorism but from laws such as these. That is the true measure of what terrorism may achieve.'

There are two sorts of control orders. One is a so-called 'non-derogating control order' because it does not derogate from (deviate from) Convention rights. This does not deprive a person of liberty but can interfere with other human rights, such as the right to privacy and to respect for family life, although the Convention allows interference if, for example, national security justifies it. A 'derogating control order' – which does deviate from Convention rights – imposes restrictions that amount to a deprivation of liberty. Before making the order a court has to be satisfied it is appropriate against a person who has been involved in terrorism. There is provision for an appeal to a court to challenge the making of an order.

Lord Phillips noted a comment by the European Commissioner for Human Rights, Alvaro Gil-Robles, who visited London in June 2005. 'He questioned whether the new legislation was compatible with Convention obligations. He suggested that the restrictions that could be imposed by non-derogating control orders might well amount to deprivation of liberty contrary to Article 5.

'He also questioned whether the provisions for review by the court satisfied the requirements of a fair trial under Article 6.'

The commissioner commented:

The proceedings fall some way short of guaranteeing the equality of arms, in so far as they include *in camera* hearings, the use of secret evidence and special advocates unable subsequently to discuss proceedings with the suspect... Quite apart from the obvious flouting of the presumption of innocence, the review proceedings described can only be considered to be fair, independent and impartial with some difficulty.[5]

Control orders were intended to replace the ordinary criminal justice system with a parallel system run by the executive. The Commissioner, and Lord Phillips by quoting him, go to the heart of the issues addressed by this book – the threat to this country's institutions by the creeping power of the State – by the executive – in a usurping of power and function.

There are dangers of MI5 becoming a parallel police force, as we have seen. We have quoted Sir Michael Jackson's complaint about the effect on the armed services. We know there are moves to control the police. Of course, terrorism has to be defeated but key measures against it are alien to a way of life and a system of justice which have been cherished over the centuries.

Britain is not a fascist state, it is a democracy, but the example of Nazi Germany shows what can go wrong without vigilance and the means to combat it. Michael Burleigh in his masterly book *The Third Reich: A New History*[6] describes the demise of the rule of law. Law in Nazi Germany, he says, was to protect and serve the collective interests of the national community rather than to defend the rights of the individual against an arbitrary executive. This fundamental characteristic of democracies was nullified in a system which fused executive and judiciary into one arbitrary identity. As the slogan had it: 'The common good precedes individual good.' The interests and values of the 'national community', as expressed through the Führer principle, became paramount: what the leader said became law. Burleigh's book is a warning of how easy it is for eloquent charismatic leaders with enthusiastic followers to inspire laws which may be at odds with European human rights safeguards. These safeguards were, of course, introduced to prevent a recurrence of the horrors of the Third Reich. In Britain the European Commissioner has noted the intrusion of the executive – an outward symptom of the Secret State.

Two much-needed defences – against imprisonment without trial and against surveillance – may have been present even before the time of Magna Carta and probably used by the Anglo-Saxons. They are reputed to have had a law against eavesdropping and are thought to have valued *habeas corpus* as a principle. Arguably eavesdropping is still an offence in common law, although no-one has been arrested for it in modern times.

Many people look on the courts as places which are there simply to punish, but they are also there to safeguard the liberty of the subject who, until the laws against terrorism, was deemed to be innocent until proven guilty. An oppressive State anxious to enforce the harsh laws it has introduced might seek to circumvent that role of the courts or restrict sentencing in a way which limited the power of the judge to judge. The tendency is endemic in modern Britain. Automatic penalties, such as for motoring offences, do away with courts, in the first instance. Old safeguards, like having to prove the accused had guilty intent, *mens rea*, are an encumbrance to mechanical justice. Mitigating circumstances are hardly relevant to a fixed penalty. The State likes people to be processed with measurable efficiency and cost-effectiveness.

This is not calculated to appeal to judges. Downgrading more offences to be dealt with by fixed penalty notices or outside the usual court system may undermine their seriousness, and judges have resisted ministerial complaints of soft sentencing when they are only following the law. They are also sensitive to any attempt to influence their sentencing for political reasons. Shortage of prison places brought about a crisis over sentencing in January 2007, which embarrassed John Reid, then Home Secretary.

Judge Richard Bray at Northampton Crown Court was reported as saying: 'I am well aware that there is overcrowding in the prison and detention centres. That is not going to prevent me from passing proper sentences in each case. The reason our prisons are full to overcrowding, and have been for years, is because judges can no longer pass deterrent sentences.'[7]

Elsewhere, one person who had previously been imprisoned was released on bail despite alleged serious sex offences against a teenager. He was put on curfew, because of concern by police about a school and to allow for a pre-sentence report. Another judge reportedly suspended a six months sentence for downloading child pornography. The Home Office had drawn attention to guidelines on alternatives to custody. An alleged cannabis smuggler was allowed to go free instead of being jailed. The judge was quoted as saying that the normal sentence would be two to three years. He preferred to keep him out rather than risk early release for someone more dangerous.

The crisis caused near panic among ministers. John Reid, Lord Falconer, the Lord Chancellor, and Lord Goldsmith, the Attorney General, urged on 23 January 2007 that only the most serious offenders should be jailed. Next day the Lord Chief Justice backed the move. Tony Blair insisted from the World Economic Forum in Switzerland: 'If any judge feels that anyone is a threat or a danger to the public, and feels that they should be put in custody, then they should be put in custody.'[8] John Reid denied interference in the judicial system with the sentencing advice, which caused confusion. He said the guidelines were issued by the Sentencing Guidelines Council, chaired by the Lord Chief Justice.

The shortage of places in prison was the result of repeated Government failure, already attacked in my book *Prison Crisis* 27 years earlier. I wrote then: 'The extent of prison overcrowding is a national disgrace.'[9]

The judges were plainly anxious to do what they were paid to do – deciding cases on their merits. The independence of judges has since been threatened by moves to lump them together with prisons in a new Ministry of Justice. Money is power, and gives power to the bureaucracy. As with the armed services, the police and hospitals, the intrusive bureaucracy is creeping ever onwards. The Ministry's budget would have to be divided between the judges and the prisons. Judges feared that might require them to take the pressure off the prison system by handing down lighter sentences. They would have to be concerned more with balancing the books than balancing the scales of justice. There could be pressure on sentencing to meet the needs of the minister rather than those of the offence and offender. If the prisons and probation service seemed short of cash, the judges could be mugged. Some courts might be forced into becoming bargain basements, letting off offenders cheaply. Lord Woolf, a former Lord Chief Justice, is one of those who thinks the courts' budget should be ring-fenced.[10]

Lord Phillips of Worth Matravers, the Lord Chief Justice, told MPs he first heard in the *Sunday Telegraph* newspaper about the creation of the Ministry of Justice. It would cause a 'serious constitutional problem'. He called for 'constitutional safeguards' to ensure the continued independence of the judiciary.[11]

Alan Beith MP, chairman of the Constitutional Affairs Select Committee, said: 'I have been in Parliament for 34 years and I don't think I have ever seen such clear anger and concern on the part of the senior judiciary.'[12]

Another example of chaos in the system was a judge's difficulties in trying to find a bail hostel place for someone who had failed for the sixth time to register as a sex offender. The hostels provide supervision of offenders who have been recently released.

Interference elsewhere by the executive in the criminal justice system worsened the crisis. Professor Rod Morgan, who resigned as head of the Youth Justice Board, said Government targets for bringing offenders to justice were swelling numbers of prisoners unnecessarily. 'Swamping' youth custody centres with inmates wrecked efforts to rehabilitate young offenders. 'I regard a 26 per cent increase in the number of children and young people that are being drawn into the system in the past three years as swamping.'[13]

Prof Morgan said that more than 80 per cent of 15–17-year-olds would be re-convicted within two years of release – and of those who had already got several convictions, the rate at which they would be re-convicted was well over 90 per cent, almost certainly. The figure proved that youth custody had a poor chance of stopping criminal behaviour. It proved that the idea of building ever more prisons to solve the crisis was 'the counsel of despair'. Prison was the 'worst environment' for many teenage offenders. More had to be invested in early preventive work with children starting to get into trouble, rather than locking up more and more of them after it was too late.

Changes facing the magistracy suggest to the detached observer that, without improvement, justice must suffer – in spite of loyalty and commitment by those providing a dedicated service, which needs better support.

- 148 magistrates' court houses closed between 1995 and 2006.
- 54 courts were in a 'critical state of repair', some of them in danger of closure at short notice for health and safety reasons.
- The courts' budget for building maintenance was being cut by 3.5 per cent every year for three years.
- Justices' clerks, who advised magistrates on the law, had been reduced in number – already from 200 to 70 in ten years. More reductions were likely.

The IT equipment in the courts was out of date. Absurdly, a system for which magistrates had long been waiting was not designed to be compatible with those used by the Crown and County Courts or police, probation and prosecution. As a result there were continuing delays in processing cases when incorrect information was provided to defence solicitors by police and prosecution, or files were incomplete or not in court. In some areas lack of money prevented the Crown Prosecution Service providing prosecutors. The cases could not then go ahead.[14]

As with the judges, budgets for magistrates' work cover conflicting demands. Magistrates are trained to be fair-minded, and are prepared to listen to the Government's case – but there could be a price to pay. We have seen in key parts of British life the increasing growth of the bureaucracy at the expense of institutions and their independence, Magistrates might like to ask themselves if they are immune, or whether they are in danger of becoming a function of the executive.

The needs of justice are coming under pressure. The Magistrates' Association says Government consultation documents openly describe initiatives in terms of cost-effectiveness rather than in terms of justice or public confidence. 'Decisions on diverting cases from the courts and increasing the use of fixed penalty notices and penalty notices for disorder are being taken on financial grounds rather than judicial ones.'[15]

Better pay to be obtained elsewhere has hit numbers of legally qualified court clerks, with the result that some cases could not go ahead. Court closures meant that victims, witnesses, defendants and solicitors had to spend more money and time on travel. Sometimes delays and adjournments were caused.

There are two ways of looking at the state of the magistracy. One is that, just as troops in battle are not always properly equipped, or hospitals have to shut wards, so magistrates have to make do with less. The other is to do with the neglect of institutions. The magistrates are an independent voice. Their loyalty must be to the law, advised by their clerks, not to the State bureaucracy.

To take an historic institution like the Privy Council and absorb its administration in the bureaucracy is a form of subversion. The magistracy is also an historic institution. *Magistrat*, a Middle English word – a civil administrator of the law – was first used in the fourteenth century. Magistrates deal with more than 95 per cent of criminal cases. They are also the people's voice in the administration of justice.

It can easily be understood by an outside observer why government initiatives might threaten morale among magistrates and damage efficiency in the criminal justice system. Public confidence in the criminal justice system is vital.

The Government's attitude is expressed in a review produced by the Home Office, Department of Constitutional Affairs and Attorney General's Office – delivery of simple, speedy, summary justice.[16] Lord Falconer argued on Sky News on 6 June 2007, that, if people had to travel to a more central court, it would help to cut delays in hearings.[17] However, Dominic Grieve, Shadow Attorney General, stated that local courts were needed to be part of the community and had in the past been easier to run. He attacked a growth of bureaucracy in the system – a complaint that is repeated in almost every part of British life. Under the latest NHS plans, people would also have to travel to central hospitals for treatment they would prefer to receive locally – just as they might prefer local justice.[18]

Seen in the context of this book, the magistracy needs to be better protected from the corrosive trends we have described. It is part of the fabric of the nation and, if the magistracy is damaged, then the nation will be too.

The next chapter will show how one threat, at least, to the judiciary and the legal process was averted. It suggests that talk of a drift to a police state may not have been so far-fetched as was believed.

6

Despotism By Stealth

Tony Blair quietly sought powers unprecedented in modern times. An innocuous sounding Bill would have allowed the Government to:

- Curtail or abolish jury trial
- Permit the Home Secretary to place citizens under house arrest
- Allow the Prime Minister to sack judges
- Rewrite the law on nationality and immigration
- Reform Magna Carta (or what remains of it).

The list was drawn up by six professors in the law faculty of Cambridge University and published in their letter to *The Times* on 16 February 2006. They say: 'It would in short create a major shift of power within the state, which in other countries would require an amendment to the constitution; and one in which the winner would be the executive, and the loser Parliament.'[1] Calling for MPs on all sides of the House to be aware of the dangers, they noted the warning also given by David Howarth, MP for Cambridge, at the second reading of the Bill.

In an article in *The Times* he made additions to the potential list of Government powers.[2] Carrying ID cards could be made compulsory, smoking in one's own home could be outlawed and the definition of terrorism altered to make ordinary political protest punishable by life imprisonment.

75

The Government's would-be 'coup' came in the guise of the Legislative and Regulatory Reform Bill which was presented as a way of getting rid of red tape by amending the Acts of Parliament that caused it. Reaction against it included a Save Parliament Campaign backed by 2,000 people. The result of combined pressure was a climb-down by the Government.

The furore came in the midst of moves by Government to curb civil liberties. John Reid, then Home Secretary, said in August 2006 that in the short-term freedoms might have to be modified to prevent their misuse and abuse by terrorists. He said the UK faced its 'most sustained period of severe threat since the end of World War II'.[3]

Earlier as Defence Secretary he had outraged human rights campaigners by using the threat of international terrorism as a reason for changes to the treatment of prisoners and the rules of war. His demand for a review of the Geneva Convention of 1949 which governs the treatment of prisoners came with his call for countries to have the right to pre-emptive strikes. He clearly hadn't thought it through. He did not say whether this could be a reason for Israel attacking Iran or, indeed, Iran attacking Israel, or even Israel attacking Lebanon. It depends what is meant by pre-emptive strikes. The militant suicide bomber might be glad to have an excuse to get in first.

MI5 has set the pace in urging a clampdown on liberties as an antidote to future terrorism. Why this should be so is not clear, since MI5 is not an elected body nor is it publicly answerable. Dame Eliza Manningham-Buller, MI5's head, was therefore speaking without democratic mandate when she gave her personal views at the sixtieth anniversary of the Dutch security service in the Hague on 1 September 2005. We have quoted her as saying there needed to be a debate on whether some erosion of what we all value might be necessary to improve the chances of British citizens not being blown apart as they went about their daily lives. The dilemma was how to protect citizens within the rule of law when 'fragile' intelligence did not mount to clear-cut evidence. Such intelligence was often not enough to support criminal charges in the courts, she said.

> We can believe, correctly, that a terrorist atrocity is being planned but those arrested by the police have to be released as the plan is too embryonic, too vague to lead to charges and possible convictions.
>
> Furthermore, such intelligence may be highly sensitive and its exposure would be very damaging as revealing either the source or our capability.

Civil liberties were valued and there was no wish to damage those hard fought for rights. 'But the world has changed,' she said.[4]

Torture, previously unthinkable, has become an issue. As we shall see in a later chapter suspected connivance at torture by some western countries has caused widespread anger. Existing safeguards against indiscriminate arrest are being disregarded. A huge inroad into liberty was made on 1 January 2006 when police were given rights to arrest people for every offence. This instantly made them vulnerable even for minor misdemeanours like failing to do up a seat belt or leaving litter.

The changes also allowed photos to be taken on the street of people arrested or given fixed penalty notices. Misused, this could lead to the creation of a national databank. The Home Office unwittingly revealed the drift of its policies by making assurances that the number of arrests would not climb, partly because fixed penalty notices were available for many offences (an issue discussed earlier in Chapter 5). Thus, the safeguards of court hearings are being undermined. Arresting officers will, however, have to be satisfied there are reasonable grounds for their actions. But who, other than the officer involved, will judge that on the spot? The constable has a big new power on a dark night in a lonely street where there are no witnesses.

Ancient rights being thrown aside were listed by the *Observer* newspaper as they stood on 23 April 2006.

- The right to trial by jury was abolished in 2003 for cases of serious and complex fraud.
- The right to protest. Since 2005, demonstrations outside the House of Commons had to be notified to the police beforehand and approved by them.
- The right not to be convicted on hearsay evidence. Such evidence could be introduced to get an anti-social behaviour order.
- The right to freedom of movement. Travel could be restricted by Cabinet Ministers in designated emergencies.[5]

The Blair Government became noted for the arbitrariness of the powers it introduced. As Hazel Blears, the then Home Office Minister, said about control orders, they were not designed to punish people for having done something wrong, but to prevent people from doing something wrong.

The enforcement of illiberal laws can produce heroes for those fighting for freedom. One such protester was Brian Haw whose campaign against war had gone on for more than 2,000 days when he won his latest legal battle to keep up his demonstration in Parliament Square. He had been charged with breaching the Serious Organised Crime and Police Act 2005. District Judge Quentin Purdy said Haw had not breached conditions imposed on him by the Metropolitan Police and that the Police Commissioner, Sir Ian Blair, rather than a junior officer, should have imposed the conditions.

The police do not like carrying out restrictive laws which are worthless and turn communities against them. Under the Terrorism Act 2000 officers were empowered to stop and search anyone within an area designated a potential terrorist target – even although they were not behaving suspiciously. Andy Hayman, an assistant commissioner of the Metropolitan Police, questioned the value of a power that caused so much pain.[6] Well-intentioned as an anti-terrorist measure, it resulted in few arrests and charges. Terrorists were very unlikely to be carrying bomb-making equipment around with them in the street, according to Mr Hayman, who was then in charge of counter-terrorism nationally.

Lord Toby Harris, of the Metropolitan Police Authority (MPA), said its research had raised serious questions over the Metropolitan Police's use of special anti-terrorism, stop-and-search powers. Of almost 23,000 stops between September 2005 and October 2006, only 27 people were held under suspicion of terrorism and another 242 were arrested for other offences.

Lord Harris, the Home Secretary's representative on the MPA, added at a London conference: 'Twenty-seven arrests producing the level of dissatisfaction, concern, anger and distance I think is something we need to look at.' He thought that the powers were probably doing more harm than good.[7]

More sinister was the power of a new anti-terrorist unit to protect Ministers, the Royal Family and others deemed to be of sufficient importance.[8] By the use of mental health laws suspects could be held indefinitely. Ten thousand people had been scrutinised to find targets – any with an obsession who could be potential stalkers or killers of leading figures. Not only psychiatrists and psychologists but police were involved in the process, which could lead to detention. The Fixated Threat Assessment Centre (FTAC) was run by Scotland Yard. Human rights activists suspected it might be a way of removing terrorist suspects without going before a court.

Law enforcement is spreading still further and is catching people previously regarded as innocent, with the banning of smoking in enclosed public places in England. It came into force on 1 July 2007. The ban included offices, factories, pubs and bars. Private homes and outdoor places would not be covered.

Simon Clark, director of Forest, the smokers' lobby, described the ban as Draconian and 'typical of a government that seems determined to interfere in every aspect of our daily lives.'[9] Health campaigners thought it would prevent the inhaling of other people's smoke, and the government forecast that about 600,000 people would give up smoking because of the new law.

It was being enforced by thousands of newly trained council

staff working under cover and spying on people. The anti-smoking police could use photography and filming if need be. They could give on-the-spot fines of £50. Owners of business premises could face fines of £200 for not displaying an adequate sign. Refusal to enforce the law could cost them £2,500. Similar bans were already in force in the Irish Republic, Scotland and Northern Ireland. Wales followed in April 2007.

Commentators against the 'nanny state' and any restriction on freedom see the smoking ban as yet another sign of the Government's heavy-handedness. A speech by the then Home Secretary, Charles Clarke, in April 2006 bitterly attacked liberal media commentators.[10] He spoke of a 'pernicious and even dangerous poison' permeating some press coverage. Clarke claimed media commentators often made 'incorrect, tendentious and over-simplified statements' about Labour's record on civil liberties.

The record, however, speaks for itself. Liberty, the civil rights watchdog, detailed some of the measures introduced during Clarke's tenure at the Home Office.

- *The Prevention of Terrorism Act 2005*. This introduced control orders, a form of punishment without trial. Because they denied the person concerned a fair trial they were declared incompatible with the Human Rights Act by a High Court judgement in April 2006.
- *The Incitement to Racial and Religious Hatred Act 2006*. This introduced significant restrictions on free speech.
- *The Terrorism Act 2006*. This doubled the time people could be detained prior to charge and brought in the offence of encouragement of terrorism, which included the issuing of statements that glorified terrorist acts. So far so good; many would approve of the latter. But the broad definition of the offence, and of terrorism, guaranteed that the reckless as well as those guilty of inciting terrorism would be swept up. It also allowed non-violent political groups to be banned.

- *The Identity Card Act 2006.* This introduced the ID card scheme and National Information Register. Liberty said such a scheme would erode privacy rights and risk damaging community relations. Research showed that where countries had ID card schemes people from ethnic minority communities were much more likely to be asked to produce their cards.

Some see these measures as signposting the way to a totalitarian state. However, Tony Blair is no Nazi – he is neither a socialist nor a nationalist. But one of the first things a totalitarian state does is to neuter the judges and undermine traditional law. The creation of Nazi Germany is an example. Michael Burleigh was quoted in an earlier chapter. He said in *The Third Reich: A New History*: 'Law was to protect and serve the collective interests of the national community, rather than to defend the rights of the individual against an arbitrary executive'[11] Blair put collective interests first against terrorist suspects. The biggest constitutional issue of the Blair administration was a clash with judges over the rights of terrorist suspects under the law.

Robust debate has been censored by petty restrictions. The criticism by a Christian couple of gay rights led to interrogation in their home by police officers for 80 minutes. The *Daily Mail* reported on 23 December 2006: 'They had dared to write to their local council about its promotion of civil partnership ceremonies and the distribution of gay rights leaflets in council buildings.'[12] The police and Wyre Borough Council apologised and agreed to pay the couple, Joe and Helen Roberts, £10,000 in compensation and £40,000 in legal costs rather than face a High Court battle over the issue of freedom of speech.

The Metropolitan Police investigated an author who said on BBC Radio Live that gay couples did not necessarily make good parents. Instances of people trying to engage in free speech include:

- A reading at the Cenotaph names of 97 British soldiers killed in Iraq. Arrested, the person concerned was given a conditional discharge by Bow Street magistrates. She was convicted of breaching a new law which banned unauthorised protests within half a mile of Westminster.

- An eleven-year-old girl was stopped and searched under the Terrorism Act. She was with her father at a protest outside Fairford air base.
- Police stopped others seeking to join the Fairford protest. Later, the Law Lords ruled the police acted unlawfully in detaining Iraq war protestors and forcibly turning them back. The Law Lords upheld the right to protest. (*Guardian.co.uk*, 14 December 2006.)

Although restrictions on free speech are deplored, there is more general support for laws aimed more accurately against terrorists, but there remains scepticism. The battle against the IRA was conducted without the need for such Draconian measures. The BBC noted on 10 November 2006 that terrorism was the cornerstone of the Queen's Speech, and John Reid, then Home Secretary, had said more legislation was needed to counter the threat.[13]

The head of MI5 had said the previous week that there were 30 terror plots active in the UK, yet recent polls had shown that there was a problem of trust and many people felt that such threats might be exaggerated.

The *Daily Mail* led the attack, quoting Dame Eliza Manningham-Buller as saying that 200 networks and 1,600 individual suspects were under surveillance, most of them British born and linked to al-Qaeda.

It seems highly convenient, to put it mildly, that her remarks come just before next week's Queen's speech, which will unveil security measures that are bound to be controversial.

Her words will also, no doubt, be used to try to bludgeon us into accepting the Government's ill-conceived and hugely expensive ID cards.

So the suspicion grows that the timing of her warning is all part of a New Labour campaign to soften up public opinion.[14]

Although people used to British ways know that someone arrested will not necessarily be charged, the statistics alarm and may alienate many in the Muslim community. Like young black people 20 years earlier on the streets of Notting Hill and Brixton, Muslims feel that they are an unfair target, perhaps for racial reasons. Figures released on 11 August 2006 showed more than 1,000 arrests under the Terrorism Act since 9/11, but 158 people charged with terrorist offences and only about 60 awaiting trial.[15]

Infringement of liberty is bad enough, but loss of life is worse. The murder of Denis Donaldson, a double agent working for British intelligence and the Special Branch, should never have happened. He ought to have been given a safe house and new identity, the least that MI5 should have done for someone who had risked his life at the top of Sinn Fein, providing information that helped to bring peace and involve the IRA in democracy.

Donaldson was recruited in the 1980s, when feeling vulnerable and compromised. In a statement in December 2005 he confessed publicly to being a double agent. Immediately he was expelled from Sinn Fein and republican circles. A journalist on the Dublin *Sunday World*, Hugh Jordan, found him in Donegal with no police protection. He was in a cottage with no running water or electricity.

Apart from being a dereliction of duty, the failure to protect him, as reported, was incredibly short-sighted. If Muslim double agents think that MI5 would abandon them to the mercies of al-Qaeda, they are unlikely to compromise themselves by revealing murderous plots.

Informers are needed if further bombing outrages are to be prevented – just as they were needed in Northern Ireland. Because of the closed nature of Muslim communities, accurate information is hard to obtain. Telephone tapping and other interception techniques are necessary, but they have to be properly used and controlled. Language presents a problem. One case of interception involved people communicating in a tongue spoken by significantly fewer than 1,000 people in the world.

This was reported by Sir Swinton Thomas, the Commissioner

responsible for policing intercepts.[16] Reading his report ought to be a reassuring, but it is not. One reason for this is a failure to substantiate arguments which he puts forward against the use of intercept evidence in criminal proceedings. The report underestimates both the terrorists in their techniques and jurors in their capacity to follow the evidence. Sir Swinton believes that the result of presenting phone tapping evidence in court would make terrorists and criminals shut up to protect themselves. However, the terrorists who bombed London were presumably not shut up, and they were not caught, although phone tapping was presumably available. The report does not recognise that any intelligent individual, let alone a terrorist, knows when not to use a telephone or when to put e-mails into cipher. Years ago I reported a criminologist's finding that knowledge of crime was based on unsuccessful criminals because they were the ones who were caught. Telephones can be used to mislead. Trade unionists used to deceive the Special Branch by giving false times and places of meetings.

Sir Swinton claims that 'criminals and terrorists do not speak in a language which is readily comprehensible to juries, even if their native language is English.' The criticisms would undermine the jury system, if true. Juries often listen to evidence in jargon, slang or dialect. I spent the first eight weeks of my national service failing to understand a recruit from remotest Scotland. Yet in another part of the report, Sir Swinton cites a case in which eavesdropping was transcribed. The work and cost in intercept cases would be very great indeed, he said. But if an interception were transcribed, the jury would have a chance to study it and discuss what was regarded as relevant. Fears that the spoken voice would cause difficulty would not then apply. Sir Swinton states:

In conclusion, in my judgement, the introduction of intercept material in the criminal process in this country (other countries have different systems) would put at risk the effectiveness of the agencies on whom we rely in the fight against terrorists and serious criminals, might well result in less convictions and more acquittals and, most important of all, the ability of the intelligence and law enforcement agencies to detect and disrupt terrorism and serious crime and so protect the public of this country would be severely handicapped.[17]

Sir Swinton does not give equal weight in his conclusion to the need for justice. If he had expressed more concern about justice, he might have seen the prospect of fewer convictions and more acquittals in a different light. They might sometimes be the right outcome. It might just be the case that intercept evidence, properly examined, could save any repetition of the sort of appalling miscarriages of justice that occurred in the cases of the Birmingham Six and the Guildford Four (see page 36).

The extra benefit to the security services of not releasing intercept evidence is that it gives them power. Smear tactics are part of their trade. Not revealing all they know allows them to make their own judgements on what may be crucial information – not the judgements of the courts, of the people or of Parliament. The real problem for MI5 is that someone might make a judgement on MI5.

The limited use of intercept evidence in court was backed by Gordon Brown, Prime Minister, after an independent review (6 February 2008). Phone tap evidence would not be used against agencies' wishes or if the evidence could have been obtained in another way.

Mr Brown told MPs 'very big hurdles' had to be cleared before the new system could be introduced, but he was confident it could become law.

The agencies have been obstructing the course of justice, and it looks as if they will continue to do so as long as they can get away with it. What other witness in a terrorist trial would be allowed to conceal evidence?

The issues to be considered by a cross-party group set up to implement the report's findings include the potential cost of transcribing e-mails and telephone conversations. Sensitive surveillance techniques would have to be protected, although if the interception were clandestine and done remotely there would have to be something wrong with the equipment or its use for techniques to be revealed. Not so computers. Methods of penetrating computers are discussed in this book. And if they are available, it would be surprising if the intelligence agencies, with their much-vaunted equipment, would not wish to use them. MPs and others who value their privacy might like to take note.

Sir Swinton favours the properly regulated tapping of the telephones of MPs and peers, who 'can engage in serious crime or terrorism without running the risk of being investigated in the same way as any other member of the public'. However, he has the greatest respect for our democratic institutions and does not think members *are* engaged in serious crime and terrorism. That respect, however, is not quite the same as defending, to the end, freedom of speech.

Sir Swinton trusts MI5 too much. As evidence in this book clearly shows, MI5 may bring undue pressure to bear on individuals in pursuing its own agenda. Telephone conversations could provide ammunition. Freedom of expression would be the loser. Talk would be more guarded. That would handicap political debate, Parliament and democracy in Britain. There was an MI5 man already at Westminster, but he was, of course, there only for security reasons, we were told. Sir Swinton's report went to Tony Blair, whose cosy relationship with MI5 was well known. Whether the independent commissioner wanted it or not, his words, although seeking honourably to be balanced and objective, could have the unforeseen and unwitting effect of encouraging the executive's case for the retention, or even advancement, of power in the Secret State.

The word *coup* is sometimes overused but two of them in recent experience have changed the nature of Britain. One more attempted coup failed. 'Coup' will be used in the next chapter as shorthand for political seizure of power by a group of insiders under a determined leader.

7

The Subverting of Britain

The mother of Parliaments is said to be an example of democratic stability to the world, but Britain is much more susceptible to coups than we like to think. Three of one sort or another have been attempted in the last 40 years, two of them producing a major change in the political life of the nation. The third, which was plotted against Harold Wilson's government in 1968, now sounds absurd and improbable. But it followed a familiar formula.

Edward Luttwak wrote in his book *Coup d'État*[1] that a coup consists of 'the infiltration of a small but critical segment of the state apparatus, which is then used to displace the government from its control of the remainder'. He was a senior fellow at the Center for Strategic and International Studies in Washington, DC.

The events of 1968 should not be dismissed completely out of hand as a kind of Ruritanian intrigue. They happened, and they are significant, not for what they failed to achieve, but by what they represent. They showed that at a time of perceived crisis forceful solutions can be conceived.

Plotting against the government was eventually brought to an end by Margaret Thatcher and Keith Joseph, her guru who was also an influential cabinet minister. They were the ringleaders of a bloodless right-wing coup within the Tory Party, which rejected consensus politics and defused the far-fetched ideas of power by some of those concerned about the decline of Britain. The coup changed the face of British politics, smashed the unions and heralded

87

a new financial accountability for state institutions.

A similar coup against the left was achieved by Tony Blair, remarked upon by a former Cabinet Secretary, Lord Wilson, in March 2007. He noted that Tony Blair and his New Labour faction had 'staged a *coup*, first against the Labour Party, and then against the processes of government'.[2]

Peter Oborne wrote in the *Daily Mail* (10 March 2007):

I have never witnessed before such an accurate summary of the trajectory of British politics over the past 13 years. In Opposition, Tony Blair and his *coterie*, began destroying the Labour Party. The link with the unions was cut, party conference was emasculated and the once-governing National Executive stripped of power.

After the 1997 General Election, the Blair clique embarked, quite deliberately, on the destruction of the defining institutions of the British State. They achieved this with huge success.[3]

The Blair coup goes further than that, using terrorism as a reason for introducing Draconian laws, undermining civil liberties and making a bid for power unprecedented, outside wartime, for a century at least.

Blair followed Thatcher in refusing to bow to the unions, Thatcher, most dramatically, with the battle against Arthur Scargill and the National Union of Mineworkers. The civil war ended with the abdication of coal as a force in Britain. The coups shifted the configuration of British politics and brought in their wake changes which sharpened antagonisms.

The events which led to the coups of Thatcher and Blair have their precedents in previous attempts to usurp power: first by Cecil King, the *Daily Mirror* tycoon; then by factions out of control in MI5 and among other right-wing activists. What happened is not simply a modern history lesson but part of a continuing revolution in British politics, which can be understood only by examining the forces at work then and now. I had gained access to MI5 by the time these conflicts first took place and, in my work with *The Times*, observed them close to. MI5's wish to influence power, and infiltrate centres of influence, is as strong as it ever was, but is today more subtle. Terrorism has provided a fresh opportunity.

My memory of the so-called 'Cecil King plot' was later rekindled by Peter Wright's book *Spycatcher*. Wright, a senior intelligence officer, wrote:

> Feelings had run high inside MI5 during 1968. There had been an effort to try to stir up trouble for (Harold) Wilson then, largely because ... Cecil King, who was a long-time agent of ours, made it clear that he would publish anything MI5 might care to leak in his direction. It was all part of Cecil King's 'coup', which he was convinced would bring down the Labour Government and replace it with a coalition led by Lord Mountbatten [the noted wartime leader and member of the Royal Family].[4]

Soon after I was appointed UK news editor of *The Times* in June, 1968, Oliver Woods, who was then a top aide in Times Newspapers, took me aside and asked me in hushed tones a strange question. Whom would I back over the issue of publicity if Mountbatten were found to have driven when under the influence of drink – Mountbatten or the editor? 'The editor,' I replied without hesitation. Oliver drifted away without further explanation or comment and I never heard him refer to it again. It was a question without an apparent context, for I had no knowledge then or since that Mountbatten had driven when under the influence. Nor was there any question of covering up such topics.

It was only after Peter Wright's revelations that I concluded that the drink-driving reference was only a metaphor, and that Oliver, in his convoluted way, was anxious to find out, as a senior member of the hierarchy, what my attitude would be if a story broke about a plot. For I was responsible, under John Grant, for all news gathering for *The Times* in the UK.

Oliver knew many influential people, as was evidenced by his memorial service. Among the names in *The Times* on 27 January 1973 of people attending were those of 'Sir Dick and Lady White'. *The Times* of 23 February 1993, reporting Sir Dick's death, said he was former head of both MI5 and MI6. He retired in 1972.

Oliver's question might have sounded vague, but its timing – soon after my June appointment – was interesting. King did not mention Mountbatten in his *Daily Mirror* statement of 10 May 1968, which was just two days after the two of them had met. King wrote:

> We can now look back nearly 25 years to the end of the war and see that this country under both Tory and Labour administrations has not made the recovery or the progress made by others, notably the defeated Japanese, Germans and Italians.
>
> We have suffered from a lack of leadership and from an unwillingness by successive Prime Ministers to make any serious attempt to mobilise the talent that is available in this once great country of ours.[5]

King attacked Harold Wilson, the Prime Minister, and called for the Parliamentary Labour Party to provide a new leader. *The Times* was among newspapers reporting the statement.

The editor, William Rees-Mogg, saw a legitimate opportunity to involve King, a subject of press interest, with *The Times* and took it. King revealed in an interview published in the *Observer* on 15 December 1968 that he had been asked by Rees-Mogg to write articles and was also receiving £7,000 for publication rights of two books of memoirs. King's book *Strictly Personal*, published by Weidenfeld and Nicolson in 1969, has a Times Newspapers copyright.

On 12 May 1969 he told the Oxford University Conservative Association that the country was leaderless. Even the Parliamentary Labour Party was beginning to see that perhaps the future would be better under almost anyone but Mr Wilson. Again there was no mention of Mountbatten.

King's comments were reported in *The Times* of 13 May.[6] He said that his *Daily Mirror* piece a year before might have played a part in his departure from the Mirror Group shortly afterwards. King was dismissed as chairman of IPC on 30 May 1968.

On 9 December that same year *The Times* carried a leading article headed 'The Danger to Britain' and providing a 'case for a coalition'. The article began:

If one is British one can only feel heart-sick about the state of the country. We know that we face an economic crisis, and that the crisis is not only economic but involves such vital matters as social discipline and the nation's will to survive. We know that Britain could perform much better, that there is no natural law which favours the Germans and discriminates against us.

The article went on:

The classic political answer is well known. In circumstances of this kind the first thing that has to be done is to restore confidence in the ability of the Government to govern. The best way to do that is to have a coalition or national government to overcome the emergency.[7]

The article gave rise to the *Observer* interview with Cecil King mentioned earlier. It began: 'Is Mr Cecil King ... the man behind last Monday's rather overheated article in *The Times* calling for a coalition?' 'Pure poppycock' was King's reply. *The Times* had not consulted him about anything. The first he knew about the leader was when he read it in *The Times*. 'I've had no discussion with them about policy. I would surmise that, if I offered my opinion or policy to them with a view to influencing them, it would probably be resented.'[8]

King was becoming a little too strident for *The Times*, which preferred to retain its own more measured tone. He was too much of a maverick to fit in, and in 1973 his contract was terminated.[9]

Mountbatten, the focus of King's plot, was used to publicity. By coincidence he was the subject of a Thames Television series and three prominent biographical articles in *The Times* which made no mention of any plot. *The Times* articles began on 31 December, very soon after the controversial leading article arguing for a coalition. Photographs illustrated the article on 1 January 1969 headed: 'The early road to fame through naval power'. Mountbatten was in uniform in three poses – as a naval cadet in 1913, as Commander-in-Chief of the Allied Forces (Mediterranean) and, most distinguished, as Chief of Defence Staff. Another photograph showed 'Admirals of the Navies of France, Greece, Italy, Turkey, the United Kingdom and the United States' pulling 'the Admiral's Galley with Lord Mountbatten in the stern on his retirement as first Commander-in-Chief, Allied Forces (Mediterranean), 1954'.

The reporter allocated to the story was Philip Howard. He wrote: 'The picture of Lord Mountbatten, hand nonchalantly in pocket, charging through the Mediterranean with his fleet, is one of his endless collection taken not by professional photographers but by ship's officers.'[10] Howard wrote that Mountbatten punctuated his memories with brisk cries of 'Got it?' and advice on writing newspaper articles.

The Times of 30 December 1968 – the day before the series began – carried details of a politically delicate report by Lord Mountbatten. It was about his post-surrender duties as Supreme Allied Commander in south-east Asia. Publication had now been authorised by the Government. An anonymous staff reporter on the paper said that publication should 'reveal much about Lord Mountbatten's powers as analyst and prophet'.[11]

The details of King's meeting with Mountbatten at his London home at 4.30 p.m. on 8 May 1968 have never been known for sure because the versions differ. A smokescreen, created no doubt in the best naval tradition, surrounds the episode. Lord Mountbatten looms out of the smoke, depicted in an apparently key role, only to slip away again, having nothing to do with it. Cecil King makes waves as he steams to and fro busily.

One example of the confusion is shown in the comments about the mood of the time made later by Lady Falkender and Harold Wilson. He is quoted in *The Times* of 30 March 1981[12] as saying that a high-level coup to take over his government had been planned in the late 1960s. He gave no firm details of the ringleaders, except to describe them as people 'high up in the press'. Wilson denied a report in *The Sunday Times* which quoted his former political secretary, Lady Falkender, as saying that Lord Mountbatten of Burma had been a prime mover.

It took time for facts to emerge. We have to see the King story in the light of what followed. In the general ferment others also had ideas about how best to deal with Britain's perceived ills. *The Times* was diligent in its scrutiny of them. An article by Brian James in *The Times* on 7 August 1987 said: 'That some elements of the military were involved in concerted or concurrent thinking about a coup is not doubted.'[13] Lady Falkender was reported as saying of the Prime Minister: 'Harold was worried when troops did an anti-terrorist exercise at Heathrow – and pointed out how easily those troops could be turned against the government.' Wilson was Prime Minister in the years 1964–6, 1966–70 and 1974–6. His fears illustrate concern about where the real power lay. There had been on 5 January 1974 just such an exercise that so worried him.

In the 1970s I became well acquainted with Sir Robert Mark, the Metropolitan Police Commissioner, and was involved in reporting police operations. Sir Robert described in his autobiography *In the Office of Constable* a possibility that terrorists had undertaken a reconnaissance of Heathrow and that they might have one or two ground-to-air missiles. He called in the army with the blessing of the Home Secretary, Robert Carr. The operation on January 5 was uneventful. Mark wrote: 'It was to be repeated quite often but with more sophistication.'[14]

Reports of the operation in *The Times* emphasised that it was controlled by the police. The paper's legal correspondent wrote on 8 January 1974: 'It has long been a principle of British law that a soldier is only a civilian in uniform. His rights are no greater than those of any citizen, except where the law has conferred them. But soldiers, like citizens, can be used to help the civil authorities, including the police, in enforcing law and order.'[15]

One reason given for the operation was that it was 'an exercise', which conflicts with Sir Robert Mark's explanation that an immediate threat was a possibility. It would not be surprising if it had really been simply an 'exercise' – but an exercise for what? I believe there was in any case a hidden agenda, and, to understand it, the operation must be seen in a wider context.

The same year as the operation at Heathrow – 1974 – *The Times* carried an article on 5 August by Lord Chalfont who, as Alun Gwynne Jones, had been the paper's defence correspondent, and, before that, a senior army officer in the War Office. The article was headed: 'Could Britain be heading for a military take-over?' Chalfont wrote:

It is worth recalling that a little more than two years ago Brigadier Frank Kitson, still a serving Army officer, was writing in a book in which the present Chief of Staff contributed a foreword: 'If a genuine and serious grievance arose, such as might result from a significant drop in the standard of living, all those who now dissipate their protest over a wide variety of causes might concentrate their efforts and produce a situation which was beyond the power of the police to handle. Should this happen, the army would be required to restore the position rapidly.'[16]

Other commentators discounted the possibility of a military take-over. However, Charles Douglas-Home, another former defence correspondent, wrote in *The Times* on August 16: 'No army, however classless and a-political, can stay like that if it is sucked into a domestic arena in a way which has already overtaken the Army in Northern Ireland and that would threaten to involve it in the UK as a whole.'[17]

Just over a fortnight later a report in *The Times* of 4 September

1974 quoted an article in *Monday World* (quarterly journal of the right-wing Monday Club) by an army lieutenant who had served in Ulster. He wrote: 'For at least two years now it has been a topic of conversation in the messes of the Army that sooner or later it would be called upon to act in England. The operations at Heathrow – three this year so far – are ominous signs that this is not just a remote possibility.' He said the Army had shown a considerable distrust of Socialist politicians. 'It has emerged, in fact, as a force that has to be reckoned with in political circles.'[18]

In the background at the time were free-lance patriotic organisations, such as Civil Assistance run by General Sir Walter Walker and other leaders. It claimed to have more than 100,000 members. Lieutenant-Colonel Robert Butler, a 58-year-old retired officer, admitted to Christopher Walker, a *Times* reporter, that a long list of names and allegations about people in Britain allegedly involved in subversive activities had already been compiled.[19]

Such reactions had already been encouraged by the power of the trade unions, particularly the miners, against the Heath Government in a fight which they effectively won.

Kitson's influential book was published in 1971. Those who wished could see in it a remarkable prescience. He was concerned lest there be a form of protest that the police could not handle. This is precisely what happened in 1972, the following year, in a clash with unions at the West Midlands Gas Board's Saltley coke depot, Birmingham, where 100,000 tonnes of coal were stockpiled. More than 60,000 trades unionists picketed nearly 100 power stations and well over 100 collieries. Flying pickets were organised by the Yorkshire National Union of Mineworkers. This hit the economy so hard that electricity output was reduced to a quarter. Industry went on to a three-day week. Pretty well all the country was hit by nine-hour power cuts. On February 10 Midland engineers on strike joined miners at Saltley, and a total of 7,000 workers faced only 500 police.

The Army meanwhile stood idly by, notably well over 7,000 troops earmarked to man 3,500 tipper lorries. Chief Constables warned that violence could result if they tried to let them through. As we have seen, this and other union disputes stoked up frustration among those who felt that orthodox party government could not cope. They were not encouraged by the prospect of a Labour Government which, in their view, might be even more pusillanimous.

A miners' ballot on 4 February 1974 showed 81 per cent wanted a strike. Three days later Heath announced an election would be held on February 28 with the idea it would have as its theme: 'Who governs Britain?' The polls forecast a Labour defeat, but Wilson won.

The Special Branch of the police would have been failing in its duty if it had not been aware of the implications as the crisis deepened in the months beforehand. Mark must have known that it would be as well if the constitutional position were made very plain, even if the threat to it were not immediate. This the Heathrow exercise certainly did, and like the best operations it had the element of surprise. Mark says in his book that he heard about a possible threat at the airport late on the afternoon of 4 January 1974, a Friday. He asked the GSO1 (General Staff Officer 1st class) of London district to get the General Officer Commanding's agreement to move troops into Heathrow by first light the following morning. He readily agreed. Contacted during the night the Conservative Home Secretary (Robert Carr) gave his blessing. Scorpion light tanks and other armoured vehicles moved in along with police, who came from two Metropolitan divisions, the Thames Valley force and the airport constabulary. Some police were armed.

Carr said later that the Prime Minister and Defence Secretary had also been involved in the decision. He added that the reason for the operation was an increase in Arab terrorist activities in Europe and the possibility that they might use stolen Sam-7 missiles. There had been contingency plans for such an operation.[20]

The febrile mood produced other side-effects. Peter Wright, the former MI5 man, alleged in his book *Spycatcher* that up to 30 members of the Security Service (MI5) had plotted to undermine the Prime Minister, Harold Wilson. Wright puts the date for the beginning of the plot as early as 1974 when Labour won the election. As we have seen, that coincided with other events relating to the country's tranquillity and constitutional well-being. What remains puzzling about Wright's allegation is why he should have made it – if he did not believe it to be true – and the detail of the evidence he provides. He was, after all, a trusted and senior member of MI5 who presumably knew how to separate fact from fiction. The job of his Service was, and is, to provide reliable intelligence. In his book Wright says he told the leader of 'the group' plotting to undermine Wilson he could not get the necessary files. 'Some of the operational people became quite aggressive. They kept saying it was the last chance to fix Wilson. "Once you've retired," they said, "we'll never get the files!" But my mind was made up, and even their taunts of cowardice could not shake me.'[21]

The 'Wilson Plot' is referred to officially in *MI5 The Security Service*.[22] It says: 'This allegation was exhaustively investigated and it was concluded, as stated publicly by Ministers, that no such plot had ever existed. Wright himself finally admitted in an interview with BBC1's *Panorama* programme in 1988 that his account had been unreliable.'

So, an account by this senior intelligence expert whose professional accuracy in MI5 was important to national security was 'unreliable'. 'Unreliable' is not the same as 'inaccurate', and we are left to wonder about the importance of the nuance. What is 'reliable'? Is an account such as *Spycatcher*'s 'reliable' only when it is officially cleared? Am I a 'reliable' journalist in the eyes of Whitehall, if I do not 'rock the boat', but am regarded as 'one of us'?

By implication, Wright had, according to his BBC interview quoted by MI5, never heard any taunts of cowardice. 'Some of the operational people' who became aggressive either never existed or, if they did so, it was only as phantoms. They have vanished in a cloud of ectoplasm, as spooks so often do.

These denials conflict, however, with other evidence, culled from the very top of MI5 itself. The quoted source is Sir Michael Hanley, then its head. Ben Pimlott, biographer of Harold Wilson, tells how concern about possible smears led Wilson to summon Hanley to ask him about them in August 1975. 'The reply he received did little to reassure him,' Pimlott writes, quoting a former adviser who remembered speaking to Wilson immediately after the MI5 chief had left. The adviser said: 'Hanley admitted that there was a small group behaving oddly or out of turn.' According to Wilson, Hanley said something like 'a small group of disaffected members'. But Hanley said they were getting back under control.[23]

There is corroboration in *Spycatcher*, by Peter Wright, who went to see Hanley in the summer of 1975 about the disaffection. 'He might have suspected that feelings against Wilson ran high in the office, but now he was learning that half his staff were up to their necks in a plot to get rid of the Prime Minister.' Hanley asked for names and Wright gave them. 'There will have to be an inquiry, of course,' Hanley said.

There is other evidence of plots to destabilise Government. It comes from Colin Wallace, an army information officer during the minority Labour Government. *The Times* had an interest in Wallace because of his professional connection with the press. Wallace maintains that he became involved with MI5 officers in Operation Clockwork Orange which was allegedly aimed at removing Harold Wilson from office as Prime Minister. Wallace said he became the target of covert operations to discredit him because of his threat to expose undercover work, forgery and homosexual blackmail of public figures in Ulster by British Intelligence.[24]

Wallace served more than six years of a ten-year sentence imposed at Lewes Crown Court for manslaughter. *The Times* reported that he was released from prison in 1986. A 16-year campaign to clear his name ended in victory in October, 1996, when his conviction for manslaughter was dismissed (quashed) as unsafe by the Lord Chief Justice, Lord Bingham of Cornhill. Wallace had consistently claimed that he was the victim of a dirty tricks campaign by MI5 to stop him from making allegations about security service operations in Northern Ireland. Wallace had received in 1990 compensation of £30,000 after an inquiry by David Calcutt QC into the Defence Ministry's handling of his dismissal.

Clinching evidence of attempts from within MI5 to undermine Labour ministers came from Lord Hunt, cabinet secretary in the years 1974 to 1979 when Labour was in power. He was in close touch with MI5. He told Channel 4's *Secret History* programme: 'There is absolutely no doubt at all that a few malcontents in MI5, who were right-wing, malicious and had serious personal grudges, were giving vent to this and spreading damaging and malicious stories about some members of the Labour government.'[25] So much for MI5's denials.

The irony is that MI5 prided itself on unearthing and watching subversives. The definition of subversion was later laid out in statute in the 1989 Security Service Act, according to Stella Rimington. It says that the job of MI5 is to protect national security 'from actions intended to overthrow or undermine parliamentary democracy by political, industrial or violent means'.

MI5, in its targeting of journalists and others, is itself subversive, as is apparent from my own personal experience and close study over many years.

Bids for power are not now so crude as in the days of Cecil King and Peter Wright. The capacity to spy on people then was not nearly so great. The extent to which it can be done these days, as shown in the next chapter, could be, if misused, a means to control.

8

Watching the People

The rebellion, when it came, shocked government ministers. Motorists, complaining about years of harassment, acted against plans to make them pay tolls for driving, which they feared would have charted their movements. All told, 1.8 million drivers backed a computerised petition against the scheme – so many, in fact, that the Downing Street web-site handling the protest crashed.

Drivers complained that a satellite or roadside beacons would track cars tagged electronically. The petition channelled indignation at further state surveillance when Britain was already one of the world's most-spied upon nations. Drivers would be charged up to £1.50 a mile at peak time with bills sent to their homes. The tracking device would cost £200 to buy. The government claimed that other means of charging could be found without intrusive surveillance.

The protesters said: 'We the undersigned petition the Prime Minister to scrap the planned vehicle tracking and road-pricing policy... The idea of tracking every vehicle at all times is sinister and wrong. Road pricing is already here with the high level of taxation on fuel. The more you travel, the more tax you pay.

'It will be an unfair tax on those who live apart from families and poorer people who will not be able to afford the high monthly costs.'

Downing Street had provided in November 2006 the means for an electronic petition to be run, to show it was keen to enhance democracy. But the people power plan backfired. The government has since shown signs of back-tracking to concentrate on local rather than national action. In an attempt to curb opposition to road pricing, drivers may be given the option of paying a toll to use a faster lane on widened motorways. (*Timesonline* 4 March 2008.)

Drivers are already seen as a means of boosting revenue for the authorities through parking meters and speed cameras. Sabotage against them has been tried. Police estimated that 400 speed cameras had been vandalised in Britain in two years. Protest became violent with a letter bomb campaign by a primary school caretaker. Miles Cooper, 27, claimed that his targets, which included the Driver and Vehicle Licensing Agency and forensic science laboratories, were turning Britain into a surveillance society.

Cooper was given an indeterminate jail sentence at Oxford Crown Court on 28 September 2007. He was told he must serve at least five years. He admitted sending seven bombs. Five of them exploded. Eight people were injured with burns and cuts. One person has permanent damage to her hearing. Cooper was found guilty on 11 charges relating to explosive devices.

Judge Julian Hall said: 'Anyone who tries through violence or threat of violence to change the political will is a terrorist and that is precisely what you did.'

Outside the court, Cooper's solicitor, Julian Richards, said his client wished to apologise to his victims and maintained he did not intend to cause the recipients serious harm. He had never sought to deny responsibility for sending the devices.

These actions were motivated by, as he perceived it, the government's concerted and ongoing efforts to control its citizens, eroding their civil liberties and hard-won freedom.

Of particular concern to him are the recent government proposals in relation to ID schemes and an extended DNA database. He can't explain why he chose to register his protest to this in such an extreme manner. All he can say is that he felt compelled to after peaceful methods that he employed were not successful.[1]

The *Independent* reported (22 December 2005)[2] that a central database installed alongside the Police National Computer in Hendon, north London, would store the details of 35 million number plate readings per day. 'These will include time, date and precise location, with camera sites monitored by global positioning satellites.' The chances of error when being monitored by a distant computer would be enormous. Each year some 250 billion miles are covered by 33 million vehicles.

Plans to give police details of journeys by millions of motorists added to fears of 'big brother' intrusion. Cameras monitoring traffic movement on major roads and city congestion were intended to give police extra means to fight crime. The move, disclosed on 17 July 2007, was condemned by Liberty as 'mass snooping'.

Concern about the intrusion into motorists' lives was matched by misgivings over a massive, £12 billion computerised system for the health service to contain patients' records. The new systems to monitor motorists and patients were a tool for the bureaucracy which was assuming control in key areas in Britain (see Chapter 1). Official assurances failed to quell fears that confidential details would be open to hackers, with the potential of causing at least embarrassment and possibly blackmail.

A combination of computer experts' confidence and Tony Blair's enthusiasm led to a new vision for the twenty-first century – a national database allowing immediate access to 50 million patients' records by doctors, nurses, paramedics and any others in the bureaucracy qualified to see them and use them. This would allow instant cross-reference – for example, to ensure drugs urgently needed for treatment in an emergency were compatible with those the patient might already be taking. Something like 30,000 or more GPs would be linked electronically by 2012 to 300 hospitals and ambulances which served them.

A poll conducted by Medix, an online healthcare research company, found that 51 per cent of GPs surveyed were unwilling to allow people's data to be included without their express permission. A national database would bring benefit to patients but there were not enough safeguards at present. The British Medical Association was worried that trust between doctors and patients could suffer without explicit consent.[3]

The health service's IT scheme was thought to be the world's biggest civil computer project. It was also turning out to be one of the most complicated to introduce. The £12.7 billion IT programme was already four years late, according to *Telegraph News* (*Telegraph.co.uk*) on 29 May 2008. Stephen O'Brien, a shadow health minister, said that the government's attempts to 'ram through a top-down, centralised, one-size-fits-all central NHS computer system' had come 'crashing down around their ears'.[4]

Such are the ramifications and implications of the project that a public inquiry is needed. Its terms of reference should include:

- Whether the project was over-ambitious and misconceived.
- Whether the means of implementing it contained fundamental flaws.
- Whether sufficient regard was paid to a need for security of the system and patients' records.
- Whether those involved in its conception and implementation were sufficiently accountable.
- Whether at all stages of the project enough was done to explain to the public what was going on.
- And whether the outcome will justify the cost.

It might be that the project would get a clean bill of health, and will be seen to be successful in every way, but the public and Parliament need to be sufficiently informed. They must judge. Projects like this tend to be fully understood only by a technocratic elite. Control must not be left to the bureaucracy – a theme of this book.

The way that patients can be put at risk was shown by an NHS computer system which wrecked 20 years of accurate immunisation records of children. *The Times* reported on 13 February 2007 that faulty software introduced in 2005 had left some primary care trusts unable to track whether children had been vaccinated and screened for genetic conditions, raising fears that many were unprotected against diseases. Parents were not being reminded when their children were due for jabs and check-ups.[5]

Such failures raised questions about the viability of patients' records in the Biggest Brother computer of them all, for the National Health Service. Not only that, but its accessibility to thousands of workers, some by their nature less diligent than others, opened up the possibility of leakage. Occasionally there are cases involving leakage of records from police computers. Crooks would be prepared to pay to get them. Sophisticated hackers these days would regard the NHS scheme as a challenge. The larger the collection of data and the more it is open to use, the greater the challenge also to computer experts using their skills and experience to keep systems safe. We have seen the ingenuity of those seeking to break into them.

The logic of an integrated database containing all personal records with access granted across Whitehall would have bureaucratic appeal. This would, if it came about, enable pension fund and television licence details to be accessed as well as motorists' records. The ultimate would be to include drivers' movements with the aim of detecting crime and to have access to hospital records if, for example, a patient was aggressive and his identity and potential for violence needed to be checked. All this might be very convenient, but it would be seen as an outrage against civil liberties. Politics is the art of the possible, however, and access to an integrated system would in theory be possible.

A succession of scandals in 2007 about breaches of data protection by official bodies involving millions of individuals' records has undermined reassurances about the safety of information that would be held in connection with controversial I.D. cards.

Britain's record for the protection of privacy is the worst in Europe, according to Privacy International, the watchdog on surveillance and privacy invasions. Its survey of 47 countries rates the U.K. as 'an endemic surveillance society' alongside Russia, the US, Singapore and China. Simon Davies, director of Privacy International, said the loss in 2007 of computer discs containing personal and bank details of 25 million UK families claiming child benefit highlighted the risks of storing information on huge government data bases.[6]

The pool of information on individuals being held electronically is showing largely unrestrained growth. Tony Blair has been a driving force, urging the logging by the State of every British adult's DNA. Asked whether numbers on the database should be restricted, he told *Sky News*: 'The number on the database should be the maximum number you can get.' There is much more personal information than in most other countries already in the computer's memory – by early 2007 3.7 million samples, equivalent to 6 per cent of the population. The *Guardian* discovered in January 2006 that 37 per cent of black men had their DNA on the data base, compared with 13 per cent of Asian men and 9 per cent of white men.[7]

A threshold has been crossed in the way technology scrutinises people. Once the scrutiny was confined to suspects. Most people did not have to have their fingerprints taken, for example. Blanket coverage has been taken a stage further with pilot lie detector tests by Harrow Council for telephone callers wanting housing and council tax benefits. A warning would tell them that they were being tested, then suspicious changes to a sample of the person's normal voice would alert staff to check in case of potential fraud.

Civil liberties have been targeted by stealth. An example was a draft proposal to use the excuse of the 2012 London Olympics to allow police greater intrusion into individual lives to help fight crime. One way would be to pick up from a DNA database family connections to single out targets. People with the same family traits might help with identification. This would merely be an extension of the power the police already have under the Criminal Justice Act of 2003 to retain DNA samples from anyone who has been arrested regardless of whether or not they were subsequently convicted. Tony Blair was greedy for more.

The UK has encouraged other governments to implement similar systems. Cross-border organisations like Interpol would be used for inter-governmental co-operation, according to Privacy International. They would be able to share and exchange the DNA profiles of their citizens. This would be subject to vague domestic legislation such as covered crime detection and prevention. 'In November 2005, the UK adopted the charter governing automated access to Interpol's database of DNA profiles.' There was little public awareness or debate surrounding the establishment of the global DNA database, which had created uncertainty about the system.

Investigation by an MP, Grant Shapps, disclosed that the DNA database included profiles of 24,000 juveniles who had never been cautioned, charged or convicted. Later the Home Office added further similar cases of 27,000 individuals who were now adults but had been arrested before the age of 18 – a grand total of 51,000. Police have been speeding up the lifetime recording of DNA samples from innocent children, reaching a total of 105,000.[8]

Commander Dave Johnston, head of Scotland Yard's murder squad said one suggestion was that DNA should be taken from babies to help solve and prevent crime.[9] Mr Johnston, who was vice-chair of the Association of Chief Police Officers' homicide working group, wanted a debate on the issues involved, including human rights. He pointed out that 'heel prick' blood samples were already taken from babies at four days to test for genetic disease. These could be used at little extra cost.

Already in June 2007 the DNA fingerprints of more than 100 children aged under ten were stored on the government database, yet they were below the age of criminal responsibility. Also recorded were 46 people more than 90 years old.

The next logical step would be to try and anticipate lethal action by potential criminals and where crimes might be committed. Risk management is a necessary science, but attempts were being made to identify the most dangerous criminals of the future – before

107

they had done anything seriously wrong. The database would include such psychological symptoms as domestic violence, mental aggression and other relevant personal history. The work was being done by the Metropolitan Police's Homicide Prevention Unit. The question is whether intervention, genuinely intended to prevent murder, would turn out to be yet another infringement of individual liberty. The safeguard of someone being innocent until proved guilty could be under threat.

A hand-held fingerprint identification transmitter is being tested by police, primarily on motorists. False names are often given by banned or uninsured drivers. More provocative would be use of the device against pedestrians, particularly if it were in racially tense areas. Much of the bad relations between police and young black people in the 1970s arose from officers acting on suspicion – 'provocatively', the black people told me. The new technology would check fingerprints from both index fingers of suspects with their permission. The image would be compared in only a few minutes with a database of 6.5 million prints. In this case, the question was whether the introduction of technology would stop there. Since more means of identification have now developed, it remained to be seen whether hand-held cameras or other more scientific tests would supplement the fingerprint tests ordered by a police officer. Roadside breath tests are already an example

While CCTV has identified terrorists and other criminals in high-profile cases, the average Londoner might be on camera 300 times each day. There were more closed circuit television cameras per head of population than in North America or any other European country. Yet a Home Office study found that 'the CCTV schemes that had been assessed had little overall effect on crime levels.'[10]

Intrusive as they are, the security measures considered necessary for protection against terrorists are to be tightened still further. The government was considering body searches and the screening of luggage at major train stations using mobile checking apparatus. Increased security is in mind for railway stations, airports, seaports and key parts of the infrastructure.

New style images would be held on identity cards. Fingerprints would be among the items on them. The fingerprints could be checked against nearly a million unsolved crimes, as Tony Blair admitted on 20 February 2007.[11]

ID cards have not found favour with Dame Stella Rimington, who retired in 1996 as head of MI5. She told the annual conference of the Association of Colleges in Birmingham in November 2005:

ID cards have possibly some purpose. But I don't think that anyone in the intelligence services, particularly in my former service, would be pressing for ID cards. My angle on ID cards is that they may be of some use but only if they can be made unforgeable – and all our other documentation is quite easy to forge.[12]

The gradual growth of electronic spying, useful as a means of solving crime, has been immense. Pioneering CCTV cameras were in Bournemouth in 1985 and senior officers spoke of its embryonic success when addressing the Police Superintendents' Association's annual conference. It began to spread. My conversations with experts pioneering DNA testing left no doubt that it was a brilliant and major innovation against crime. But as is often the case, the device itself is morally neutral. The benefits – and dangers – lie in the use to which it is put.

The beginnings of real concern about threats to liberty from intrusive technology had originated more than 30 years ago from an extraordinary source – Professor R.V. Jones who made one of the most valuable scientific contributions to Britain's effort in the Second World War. Technological intelligence was his field, and he knew what he was talking about.

He found out how to identify and jam Luftwaffe radio beams which, when they intersected, told the bomb-aimer he was over the target. Following British interference with the beams, the aircraft dropped their bombs over the countryside instead of on cities. He was involved in the use of double agents to send back false reports of hits by V1 bombers, so that the range was shortened and they missed London. In co-operation with photo-reconnaissance airmen he identified a sophisticated German night interception system, laying it open to RAF attack. A Combined Service raid on Dieppe seized secret enemy devices and an operator. Jones's alertness to a warning from a brave French resistance fighter about pilotless German aircraft led to 1,300 US aircraft dropping 1,700 tons of bombs on enemy rocket sites. Lives were saved on D-Day when, on Jones's advice, the allies destroyed virtually all German radar stations in north-west France. The real allied assaults were concealed as part of an elaborate deception plan.

Deception is also used in surveillance. When Professor Jones was Director of Scientific Intelligence at the Ministry of Defence he and the Americans knew of a Russian bugging device, built into a model of the great seal of the United States and presented to the American ambassador in Moscow.

It was highly significant that a scientist with his foresight and concern for the freedoms he had fought for should devote himself to opposing emerging threats to liberty. He made his concern, way ahead of his time, apparent to me, for *The Times*, at a Council of Europe conference on safeguarding privacy as long ago as 1970.[13]

He told the conference that the United States were said to have a microphone that, complete with transmitter, could be fired as a dart from a gun. By using a laser beam, it was possible to pick up the vibrations of a window pane caused by people talking in a room, and monitor their conversation. It was already possible to modify the behaviour of animals by sending signals to electrodes implanted in the brain, and it might therefore be possible to do the same with human beings. We could easily face the possibility that the entire development of an individual could be determined by feeding him or her on the right materials in infancy, just as bees can determine by feeding whether they rear a worker or a queen. Although computers, as known today, had yet to sweep the world, Professor Jones said that a laser system in existence, with 10 reels each containing 1,500 metres of tape 2.5 centimetres wide, could store a 20-page dossier on every man, woman and child in the world.

The ultimate fear, more out of science fiction than reality, was that one could be criminally under the control of someone else. Yet this actually happened to young girls who fell victim of a computer hacker. Having received their e-mails via a chat room, he threatened to crash their computers. He blackmailed them into stripping and sending revealing poses of themselves. He was jailed for 10 years.[14]

The way the hacker operated provides an instructive insight into the power that can be exerted over personal computers. His victims saw he was taking control of them, switching on printers, moving cursors as he wished. The court heard that a bogus photograph he sent contained a secret virus which gave him remote control of the victim's computer. He told one frightened girl he knew she had sent a message to someone else.

If that sort of intrusion is possible it must be of use to intelligence agencies, such as MI5. It is shown to be not only a weapon with which to discover what a computer operator is up to but to be used by the unscrupulous to disconcert and intimidate. In the wrong hands it could be a tool for blackmail, and not only to induce young girls to succumb to indecent demands. MI5's interest in technology is well known.

Alan Burkitt-Gray, editor of *Global Telecoms Business*, a publication of the Euromoney Goup, suspects that Government spies, like GCHQ and the intelligence services, could create permanent pathways into computers, perhaps with the knowledge of co-operative internet service providers. He says that the new technology follows on from telephone tapping of the 1960s. Digital advances have changed a system in which clumsy clicks and interference on the line might have alerted the target caller. Conversations can be copied without the exchange or the computer network being aware of it, and the signal does not degrade.

Greater Manchester Police issued a warning in May 2006 to all computer users about the need to protect themselves against rogue operators gaining access to their screens. These remove bills, letters and other personal details, and then demand money to return them. So-called 'cookies' can act as spying agents in your computer and are intended to see what you are doing there, often without your knowledge or agreement. The next stage will be a more pervasive system to identify key-strokes and thus follow writing as it takes place. Laws preventing infringement of privacy are more difficult to frame and enforce in a global system like the internet, which crosses frontiers and is used by ever more powerful and intrusive systems.

E-mail leaves a trail. 'It's like sending a postcard from computer to computer,' says Alan Burkitt-Gray. 'It is stored on every computer it goes through, and it can be copied anywhere along the line, without your knowledge.'

The intrusiveness of intelligence agencies has been boosted by a spying system enabling all phone calls, faxes or e-mails from anywhere in the world to be monitored. Code-named Echelon, details of it have gradually emerged over the past ten years. Eavesdropping stations involved include the US military base at Menwith Hill, in North Yorkshire. A global network links the US National Security Agency at Fort Mead in Maryland, and listening posts around the world. Britain's GCHQ is part of the system.

My conversation with one of my collaborators for this book, reported earlier, tested third-party reactions to key words on the telephone. It resulted in the call being interrupted when 'coup d'état' was mentioned. There is, of course, no corroboration that Echelon was involved: the evidence is circumstantial but pertinent. An alert is triggered by key words or patterns of words in the myriad messages being scanned by Echelon. Individual voices can be identified electronically. The immediate aim is to pick up signs of terrorism or other international crime.

The existence of Echelon was confirmed by a report commissioned by the European Parliament in 1997. Monitoring was routine and indiscriminate, the report said. The story had been reported by Duncan Campbell in the *New Statesman* on 12 August 12 1988, when he described plans for the system. Agencies involved in the network would be from Britain, Australia, Germany and Japan – and, surprisingly, the People's Republic of China.[15]

By 2001 the European Parliament had woken up to the need for Europeans to protect themselves against Echelon. Its report warned on 29 May that they should use more encryption as a protection. Gerhard Schmid, the European Parliament's vice president, said of the global intercept network: 'They do tap into private, civilian and corporate telecommunications.'

MI5 and other security and intelligence agencies in Britain are Echelon users. They can intercept e-mails sent and delivered without having to apply for a warrant, under the Regulation of Investigatory Powers Act. Keys to encoded e-mails would have to be handed over by users on demand.

The remarkable scope of the Act can be seen in its long title which says it is to make provision for and about:

- The interception of communications
- The acquisition and disclosure of data relating to communications
- The carrying out of surveillance
- The use of covert human intelligence sources
- The acquisition of the means by which electronic data protected by encryption or passwords may be decrypted or assessed.

The *Guardian* (30 May 2001) quoted James Bamford, a US authority on the National Security Agency, as saying in his book *Body of Secrets* that, unchecked, Echelon could become a 'cyber secret police without courts, juries, or the right to a defence'. The *Guardian* said there was no redress against the use of intrusive technology by US and EU agencies.[16]

Echelon is, however, only one of an expanding range of intrusive surveillance, which the honest citizen finds difficult to escape. Even if he hides in the wildest and remotest countryside and uses his mobile telephone, his position will be known; as it must have been when I phoned home from the higher slopes of Ben Nevis. The watchers and their analysts can find out where you go, what your habits and preferences are and, if you travel to a city, can see your picture relayed from cameras as you go about your visit. Typically you will be noticed by a camera up to 300 times a day. No other country has so many public CCTV cameras – one in Britain for every 14 people, or 4.2 million in total.

No other country spies upon its citizens more, according to a report compiled on behalf of the Information Commissioner, Richard Thomas, Every internet site they go to is recorded. Identity cards will enhance the tracing of their movements and when they use a public service.

It is the combination of databases which provides so much potential power over individuals. A study of the surveillance society which Mr Thomas commissioned in 2006[17] said: 'The combination of CCTV, biometrics, databases and tracking technologies can be seen as part of a much broader exploration, often funded with support from the US/UK "war on terror", of the use of interconnected "smart" systems to track movements and behaviours of millions of people in both time and space.'

The study disclosed the hazards that may be caused to individuals as a result of information held on them.

One inadvertent or ill-advised key stroke can easily cause havoc. Think of the release for 'research' purposes of 20 million of ordinary people's on-line search queries from AOL in August 2006. Supposedly shorn of identifiers, it took only moments to start connecting search records with names.

The research, by the Surveillance Studies Network, showed how data could be used to profile people. Use of credit cards, mobile phone calls and other sources traceable to a person were combined with additional data from loyalty cards, customer surveys, focus groups, promotional contests, product information requests, call centre contacts, website cookies, consumer feedback forums and credit transactions. The use of postal codes enabled street populations to be profiled – for example, as 'prudent pensioners'.

The Network noted that all new systems for ID cards and passports used some kind of biometrics: fingerprints, iris-scans, facial topography and hand scans. Data and information could then be fixed to the identity provided by the human body – and called up. The Network's study had a worrying, unstated implication. Since research into facial recognition was under way, it should in due course be possible to identify automatically individuals walking in the street and link them to data held about them.

Microsoft is reportedly developing the ultimate in electronic scrutiny – software capable of remotely monitoring a worker's productivity, physical wellbeing and competence. *The Times* said it had seen a patent application filed by the company for a computer system that links workers to their computers via wireless sensors that measure their metabolism. The system would allow managers to monitor employees' performance by measuring their heart rate, body temperature, movement, facial expression and blood pressure. If the system picked up an increase in heart rate, or facial expressions suggestive of stress or frustration, it would tell management that he or she needed help.[18]

It is already possible to track people, vehicles or commodities using RFID (radio frequency identification). Smart tags encoded with computer memory, when attached, can be read by radio at a distance. Tags could be used for monitoring people, as well as commodities. Stores are beginning to introduce the smart tags on goods. Shoppers could find themselves secretly tracked by RFID.

A consultative study throughout Europe of RFID, carried out by the European Commission, was disclosed at the Cebit technology fair in Hanover. One of its principal apostles, Vint Cerf, of Google, foresaw a future in which radio tags would be so widespread that they could find a missing sock, even if it were under a sofa or trapped in a washing machine.[19]

Viviane Reding, EU Commissioner for Information Society and Media, said: 'We are heading towards a world in which billions of networked objects and sensors will report their location, identity and history.'[20] However, they would not be allowed to undermine fundamental liberties that European citizens enjoyed.

Those prominent in the field are anxious to emphasise safeguards against misuse and any potential danger to civil liberties. However, it takes little imagination to see the attraction of RFID for covert intelligence organisations. For them it would be possibly the most useful tracking device of its kind ever invented.

Another hidden threat to civil liberties has come from increasingly popular pre-paid Oyster travel cards, used to avoid ticket machines and kiosks. Owners can be tracked by the data trail of personal details they leave. Police were granted access 229 times out of 243 applications they made.

Merely using a computer may provide a record of your interests as disclosed by the searches you make. Tightened security has demanded more information about airline passengers, but this has made more of it available, as Steve Boggan reported in the *Guardian* on 3 May 2006.[21] A discarded British Airways boarding pass stub gave the passenger's name, seat number, flight number and where he had flown from. His frequent flyer number was also included. Boggan and a computer expert, Adam Laurie, logged on to BA's web site and bought a ticket using the name on the stub. With the aid of the passenger's frequent flyer number – a password was not needed – full access to his personal details was obtained. This included his passport number, the date it expired and his date of birth. Using his personal details with which to surf publicly available databases, Boggan and Laurie took only 15 minutes to discover where the passenger lived, who lived there with him, where he worked, which universities he had attended and how much he had paid for his house.

Spying becomes ever more bizarre. Teignbridge District Council sent leaflets to householders urging them to spy on each other if they did not use rubbish collections properly. The leaflet read: 'It is now easier than ever to recycle, yet 30 per cent of residents still aren't. Do you know of someone in your road who is not doing their bit? Do you feel strongly enough about it to let us help them? Then contact us free on … and a recycling sheriff will be there to assist.' Leaflets had gone to people in towns in parts of Devon.[22] Another new council initiative was to fit bugs to wheelie-bins. They could tell the weight of rubbish collected, and other uses are feared – the most bizarre spying in the surveillance society so far.[23]

The State is extending its scrutiny even to future citizens. Intervention will come before birth, to prevent trouble for children later on. The government was drawing on New Zealand research which showed that children born into the most deprived households were 100 times more likely than well placed children to get into difficulty at the age of 15 over drink, teenage pregnancy, drugs, crime and hooliganism. Midwives would be the sentinels, taking the initiative in calling for help to save mothers from pressures such as family breakdown and other destructive troubles.[24]

Liberty, the independent human rights organisation, says: 'We seem to be moving from a society where information isn't shared unless there is a specific reason it should be, to a society where all information is shared unless there is a reason it should not be.'[25]

Nothing more vividly expresses the control exercised by the authoritarian state than the voice given to the all-seeing CCTV camera – the voice of a watching monitor. People who did wrong in the eyes of the watchers might be startled to hear the voice telling them so. Throwing down litter was an example. Their sins would be transmitted to a control room playing God and, while only God might strike sinners with lightning and a clap of thunder, their sins would find them out, and a voice sound from on high – as high as the loudspeaker, that is. Middlesborough began exercising this big brotherly power, and other places were eagerly taking it up. If you disobeyed the voice you might be photographed and punished.

The ultimate intrusion is by officials with power to enter your home. Many more powers have been granted under statute now –

117

an extra 60 in the 1980s and 1990s compared with only 10 in the 1950s. There were in total 266 ways in which the State could enter your home, said Harry Snook, a barrister. His study, *Crossing the Threshold*, 21 April 2007, was written for the Centre for Policy Studies. He said:

> Many powers are drafted so broadly that the citizen has little or no protection if officials behave officiously or vindictively. Some carry Draconian penalties for obstruction, including heavy fines and prison sentences of up to two years.
>
> Force can be used in the exercise of almost all these powers. In part this is due to its specific authorisation by law; in part to the courts' readiness to imply a right to use force on grounds of necessity.[26]

Some surveillance would be welcomed by many, but not the blanket coverage which deprives people of a right to anonymity or treats them all as suspects. Misinterpretation of information can place liberty in jeopardy – a mockery of the ancient safeguard of *habeas corpus*.

In the Second World War when the fight was for freedom, government posters warned: 'Careless talk costs lives.' Careless talk or behaviour these days could wreck your own life.

Spying can destroy people. The ultimate and inhuman sanction against suspects is torture, as the next chapter will show. Those who talk up the peril the West faces and spend more money on dealing with it want results, and the biggest result of all in this authoritarian age has been detention at Guantanamo Bay.

9

Torture – A War Crime

As a result of official disclosures, more is now known about the harsh treatment of detainees kidnapped as terrorist suspects. The key evidence is so revealing that it will be provided here at length and in detail, with little editing, so that the reader can see the implications for himself or herself. The question facing Britain from the facts presented here is: has a war crime been committed?

The first official indication that information obtained from tortured detainees could have been passed to MI5 came from Dame Eliza Manningham-Buller, its then Director General, in a statement on 20 September 2005, to a Law Lords hearing.[1] She did not refer specifically to torture but to 'detainee reporting', as a result of which foreign authorities had provided information, and it had proved to be very valuable in disrupting terrorist activity.

Her statement is a key to understanding MI5's attitude – and therefore that of the British government – towards the sustained concern here and abroad about the legality of using information from client states prepared to employ torture to obtain it. Using the results of torture abroad would avoid law-breaking at home, although the pain for the tortured would remain. Should such information be used, it would be a small step then if suspects were flown out to be tortured on behalf of the 'war against terror'. The question is, did Britain turn a blind eye to flights using the country for the onward transport of prisoners against their will to be tortured? Or did MI5 collude with the CIA in shipping out residents in

Britain to the notorious Guantanamo Bay? The issues involved are of a kind not considered in the West since the Nuremberg trials.

If it could be proved the British government knew the details of the flights and their purpose, or connived at them, there would be a risk that they could be guilty of war crimes, according to a general statement on the legalities involved by Lord Steyn, a Law Lord. A Council of Europe investigator suggested secret services might have collaborated without telling their governments.

Given the seriousness of the allegations, it is appropriate to report in full a relevant part of what Dame Eliza said:

Intelligence received from foreign intelligence services can originate from a wide range of different sources, human and technical. However, its provenance is often obscured by the foreign service in order to protect sensitive sources or to comply with local legislation.

Where circumstances permit, the agencies will, of course, seek to acquire as much context as possible, particularly if the intelligence is threat-related. However, our ability to do this effectively is often limited. Even if the foreign intelligence service is not prevented from disclosing such information by local legislation, it will usually decline to provide it in order to protect its source. In such circumstances, the agencies will generally not press to be told the source, as to do so would be likely to damage co-operation and the future flow of intelligence from the originating service. Further, some foreign services, especially those with whom the liaison relationship is less mature, will often provide access to 'liaison officers' rather than to operational staff. These liaison officers will be working from tightly defined briefs and will often not be in a position to provide further context.

Where more context can be obtained it may assist the agencies in assessing the reliability of the reporting. However, where the reporting is threat-related, the desire for context will usually be subservient to the need to take action to establish the facts, in order to protect life. Most credible threat-reporting received by the agencies requires immediate action. Often there is no specific timetable attached to the reporting, but public safety concerns dictate that the agencies work from a position of possible imminence. The need to react swiftly to safeguard life precludes the possibility of spending days or weeks probing the precise sourcing of the intelligence before taking action upon it, especially when such probing is in any event unlikely to be productive.

In some cases, it may be apparent to the agencies that the intelligence has been obtained from individuals in detention ('detainee reporting'), though, even then, the agencies will often not know the location or details of detention. We treat such intelligence with great care, for two main reasons: detainees can seek to mislead their questioners, and where the agencies are not aware of the circumstances in which the intelligence was obtained, it is likely to be more difficult to assess its reliability. However, experience proves that detainee reporting can be accurate and may enable lives to be saved.[2]

So, in other words, don't ask too many questions, take action and the end, within reason, justifies the source – an attitude which could have more general implications for the way MI5 regards itself and operates. Dame Eliza's comments were seen by Channel 4 News.

Any link between MI5 and what American intelligence calls 'extraordinary rendition' was not apparent in Dame Eliza's document. The term means the seizing of a suspect who is not put on trial but flown to a country where torture is known, out of sight of the International Committee of the Red Cross and with no lawyer to represent him. The pattern emerged in 2005, when countries alleged to participate included Egypt, Syria, Morocco, Uzbekistan. and Afghanistan.

Craig Murray, the former British Ambassador to Uzbekistan, was reported by the BBC (12 December 2005) as saying it was untrue that the UK Government did not use information from torture. He had been told that the UK did not use torture itself or ask that any specific person be tortured. 'As long as we kept within that guideline, then if the Uzbeks, or the Syrians or the Egyptians or anyone else tortured someone and gave us the information that was OK,' Murray said.[3] He was speaking as controversy about extraordinary rendition mounted. The Law Lords ruled that secret evidence that might have been obtained by torture could not be used against terror suspects in the courts.

Significantly, Lord Carlile, the independent reviewer of the Government's terrorism laws, said that evidence in a small number of cases would now be re-examined.

In a forthright ruling, Lord Bingham, the former Lord Chief Justice, one of a panel of seven law lords, said English law had abhorred torture and its fruits for more than 500 years. 'I am startled, even a little dismayed, at the suggestion (and the acceptance by the Court of Appeal majority) that this deeply-rooted tradition and an international obligation solemnly and explicitly undertaken can be overridden by a statute and a procedural rule which make no mention of torture at all.' He was joined in his criticism by Lord Carswell, who said that allowing evidence from torture to be used would involve the State in moral defilement.[4]

Before considering whether the US and British governments are culpable, it is necessary to considerwhat 'rendition' and 'extraordinary rendition' actually mean. International laws do not cover them. They are a convenient term for practices causing anger and dismay. Extraordinary rendition' arouses most concern.

'Rendition', on the other hand, is meant to infer that torture is not involved. Suspects are ghosted out to other countries using methods outside normal legal practice. Rendition is a convenient word for use by governments and politicians.

Western governments would not say explicitly that torture was involved, but their use of the term 'rendition' arouses deep suspicion among human rights observers.

Torture methods are said to include slaps, sleep deprivation, forced standing, exposure to cold and 'waterboarding', in which interrogators immerse or pour water over a detainee's face until he believes he will suffocate or drown. Human Rights Watch, on 21 November 2005, is quoted in a House of Commons library note as equating the torture to a mock execution.[5] Corroboration is difficult.

Robert Baer, a former CIA agent, is quoted in the same note as saying: 'If you want a serious interrogation, you send the prisoner to Jordan. If you want him to be tortured you send him to Syria. If you want them to disappear... You send them to Egypt.[6]

The same note cites a report by Senator Dick Marty, a Council of Europe investigator. He said documents had been forwarded to him by Craig Murray, former British ambassador to Uzbekistan. They appeared to be damning for the UK authorities, which seemed to have knowingly continued to make use of information obtained under torture and supplied by the Uzbek intelligence services.[7]

Human Rights Watch, Baer and Marty are quoted in a note for the benefit of MPs and their staff. It is by Adèle Brown, a research library clerk with the House of Commons Library.[8]

As ambassador from August 2002 to October 2004, Murray saw intelligence material passed to the CIA by Uzbek Security Services, he says on his website.

Murray's statement is given in detail below to show the true attitude of the Foreign and Commonwealth Office (FCO) to torture. It can be compared with MI5's description, given earlier.

I had learnt a great deal about the *modus operandi* of the Uzbek security services and their widespread use of torture. I sent my deputy, Karen Moran, to see the US Embassy in Tashkent to check if my fears about the origin of the intelligence material might be justified. The head of the CIA station confirmed to her that the material probably was obtained under torture, but added that the CIA had not seen this as a problem.

In November 2002, late January or early February 2003 and finally June 2004 I sent official telegrams to the FCO stating that I believed we were receiving material from torture, that the material was painting a false picture and that it was both illegal and immoral for us to receive it.

In March 2003 I was summoned back to the FCO and told by Sir Michael Wood, chief legal adviser, that it was not illegal under the UN Convention Against Torture for us to obtain or to use intelligence gained under torture, provided we did not torture ourselves or request that a named individual be tortured. [This can now be compared with the Law Lords' ruling.][9]

Murray said he had not heard the phrase 'extraordinary rendition'. nor was he a first-hand authority on it. 'What I can confirm is the positive policy decision by the US and UK to use Uzbek torture material.'

On 23 December 2005 the BBC reported that an Italian Court had issued Europe-wide arrest warrants for 22 suspected CIA agents accused of helping to abduct a Muslim cleric in Milan in 2003 without the knowledge of the Italian authorities. They are alleged to have then flown Osama Mustafa Hassan, also known as Abu Omar, to Egypt for interrogation. He reportedly called his family later saying he had been tortured with electric shocks during his detention.[10]

A German court issued arrest warrants in January 2007 for 13 suspected CIA agents. Khaled el-Masri, a German national of Lebanese background, said he was tortured during five months in an Afghan prison. He wanted to sue the CIA. The thirteen suspected CIA agents were alleged to have kidnapped him.[11]

An Ethiopian student who had lived in London, said he was nearly three years in the CIA's secret sites.[12] He claimed that British and US intelligence agencies were involved. Captured in Pakistan, he said he was warned by British officials he would be taken to a country where torture was used. In July 2002 he was moved to Morocco on a CIA flight and tortured, he said. His questioners knew details from his seven years in London, including the name of his kick-boxing teacher. His lawyers believed there were British sources for the information.

President George Bush has cited the London bombings to justify his support for waterboarding. He told the BBC in an interview broadcast on 14 February 2008 that information obtained from alleged terrorists helped save lives, and the families of victims of the London bombings would understand that. He said that waterboarding, which simulates drowning, was not torture. He was threatening to veto a congressional bill that would ban it. Claiming that the US upheld human rights, he defended the existence of Guantanamo Bay.[13]

Increasing allegations by European politicians and human rights bodies that international laws were being broken in 'the war on terror' added force to a landmark interview by Jon Snow with Lord Steyn, published by Channel 4 News on 6 December 2005. Lord Steyn said the true definition of torture included coercive questioning. He said the need for human rights law had been increased, not lessened, by the events of 9/11 and since.

> We have seen a scale of lawlessness unravel which in my opinion is the logical extension of Guantanamo Bay, because Guantanamo Bay involved taking prisoners from Afghanistan and many other places to an island where there would be a lawless black hole where they can never escape from... This logically is not very different from what the Americans call rendition which is, in truth, abduction.[14]

The movement of people around the world from one detention centre to another was not legal. A statement by the British Defence Secretary (Geoff Hoon) that Guantanamo Bay was legal was 'a very surprising thing for the British Government to have said'.

Jon Snow then asked what the cumulative effect was of Guantanamo Bay, of removal and black sites, of not declaring where people were held. Lawlessness on a truly grand scale, said Lord Steyn...

'If prisoners are tortured at Guatanamo Bay or at black sites – if they are – those who commit those acts will be guilty of war crimes.'

But what about the landing of a plane or knowledge of the passage of an individual, Jon Snow asked, inviting an answer on rendition. Did that amount to a war crime?

'It's going to depend on degree. But once there is knowledge that the detainees may be tortured there is a risk that those who facilitate these flights may be guilty.'

Jon Snow: 'Let me press you then: the British authorities may be guilty of war crimes?'

Lord Steyn: 'If the British authorities were fully aware of the purpose of the flights; if they were aware that these were attempts to take detainees to a place where they could be tortured, of course there is a risk that the British authorities may themselves be guilty of war crimes. But it is dependent of proof.'

Governments in Europe did know something, if not enough to judge, according to Colin Powell, the ex-US Secretary of State. He told the BBC (17 December 2005) that the practice of rendition, moving people to places where they were not covered by US law, was neither 'new or unknown' to Europe. Procedures to deal with such people had been in place over the years.[15]

The accusations began to point at national secret services. Dick Marty, the Swiss senator probing allegations of secret CIA prisons for the Council of Europe, said in December 2005 he believed collaboration between European secret services had gone well beyond exchanges of information. 'I think it would have been difficult for these actions to have taken place without a degree of collaboration. But it is possible that secret services did not inform their governments.'[16]

Senator Marty said in a report to the Council that claims about the flights were credible. There were indications that the CIA had abducted and illegally transported terror suspects across European borders. His investigation concluded on 8 June 2007 that the CIA ran secret prisons in Poland and Romania from 2003 to 2005. Marty's report said that NATO signed an agreement after the 9/11 attacks allowing the CIA to fly civilian jets through members' air space under its extraordinary rendition programme. Marty said that the highest state authorities were aware of the CIA's illegal activities on their territories. Collaboration by allies of the United States was within the structure of NATO's security programme. The prisons allowed interrogation of terrorism suspects outside US legal constraints. Critics have condemned as torture the treatment many are said to have received. A spokesman of the CIA and politicians from Romania and Poland have denied the report's findings.

A finding by the Association of Chief Police Officers that Britain did not allow extraordinary rendition flights to use its airports to take away suspects led to a clash with Liberty, the human rights organisation, and 'proof' in the *Mail on Sunday* (10 June 2007) which contradicted police claims. The *Mail* picture showed an aircraft said to have been involved in 'ghost' flights approaching RAF Mildenhall in Suffolk. Shami Chakrabarti, Liberty's director, is quoted as saying: 'ACPO have admitted to me in a private letter that their investigation amounted to little more than a cursory review of reports on the issue – which they issued, 18 months after I requested it, to coincide with the Council of Europe's report.'[17] ACPO and the Foreign Office spokeswomen both issued denials in response to the claims.

An all-party parliamentary group on extraordinary rendition attacked Jack Straw's statement that there were no records of the CIA flying terror suspects via the UK to be tortured. The statement may be 'worthless', the group said. It had been established on the initiative of Sir Menzies Campbell MP, Liberal Democrat, and Andrew Tyrie MP, Conservative. Mr Tyrie said there were no records, because they were not kept, according to the Home Office, once the transit was completed.[18]

Called in by the group for legal advice, James Crawford, professor of international law at Cambridge, said: 'A Government is not exonerated from conduct which leads directly to a person being tortured merely by closing its eyes to that prospect.'

David Milliband, the British foreign secretary, was forced to apologise on 21 February 2008, for incorrect assurances that secret CIA rendition flights did not land on British soil. Two landed on the British overseas territory of Diego Garcia in the Indian Ocean to refuel at US facilities there. In both cases a single detainee was on board. Record errors were blamed by the Americans for failure to notify Britain earlier.[19]

In fact, British agents were known to be among the groups of foreign operatives working with a core of US intelligence case officers in counter-terrorism operations. They formed part of the 'Alliance Base', believed to be in France, details of which were given in the *Washington Post*.[20] Foreign intelligence services worked alongside the agency. The *Post* story showed how the base allowed joint work by operatives from different countries without being compromised by obvious ties to the rendition programme. The working language was French to help distance them from US influence. The base was under the command of a senior French officer. It chose a lead country for each operation, and that country's service ran the operation.

Such joint intelligence work was responsible for identifying, tracking and capturing or killing the vast majority of committed *jihadists* who had been targeted outside Iraq and Afghanistan since the September 11 attacks, according to terrorism experts.

Details were given to the *Post* by six US and foreign intelligence specialists involved in its work. The multinational base was unique in planning operations, instead of merely sharing information between countries. 'It has case officers from Britain, France, Germany, Canada, Australia and the United States.'

One of the most exhaustive investigations into 'illegal CIA activities in Europe' was by a committee of the European Parliament. The Committee's final report, on 14 February 2007,[21] accuses European countries of turning a blind eye to flights operated by the CIA which 'on some occasions were being used for extraordinary rendition or the illegal transportation of detainees'. In some cases, the report says, 'temporary secret detention facilities in European countries may have been located at US military bases'.

The Government of the United Kingdom was, with four others, specifically criticised for 'unwillingness' to co-operate with the

European Parliament's investigations, but the criticism was removed after intervention by Labour MEPs.

The report states: 'At least 1,245 flights operated by the CIA flew into European airspace or stopped over at European airports between the end of 2001 and the end of 2005.' Not all the flights had been used for 'extraordinary rendition'.

MEPs cite up to 21 well-documented cases of extraordinary renditions in which victims were transferred through a European country or were residents in a European State at the time of their kidnapping.

The European Parliament slates extraordinary renditions as 'an illegal instrument used by the USA in the fight against terrorism'. MEPs condemn 'the acceptance and concealing of the practice on several occasions by the secret services and governmental authorities of certain European countries.' In the light of the available evidence there was 'a strong possibility that some European countries may have received ... information obtained under torture.'

Bearing in mind Lord Steyn's opinion about the risk of war crimes, the question is whether Britain is guilty of this, or at least conniving with the United States in illegal renditions. Two British residents ended up in Guantanamo Bay after an MI5 man called at the house of one of them, Jamil el-Banna, and interviewed him. He and Bisher al-Rawi intended to travel to The Gambia to set up a peanut oil factory.

According to a series of telegrams disclosed by Reprieve, which represents the people affected, MI5 contacted US intelligence, 'spoke at length about this operation' and then, on 8 November 2002, sent an urgent message concerning Mr el-Banna's flight details. 'We are able to confirm that ... [Jamil el-Banna and Bisher al-Rawi] have today boarded Sierra National Airline Flight LJ054 to Banjul, Gambia. The flight was due to depart from the UK at 1230 but the departure was delayed until 1310.'[22]

Reprieve states: Mr el-Banna and Mr al-Rawi were duly detained at the airport in The Gambia, turned over to the US, rendered to the Dark Prison in Kabul for several months and then taken to

Guantanamo Bay. There Mr el-Banna was held for five years before his return to Britain.

Clive Stafford-Smith, Reprieve's legal director, commented:

The British government takes the position that it played no role in the detention and rendition of Mr el-Banna. This position is simply untenable in light of the evidence. It is clear that British officials encouraged ... Mr el-Banna to travel on his wholly innocent business trip to The Gambia, and then actively worked with the US to effectuate his detention and rendition to Afghanistan and Guantanamo.

Documented evidence has been cited in support of the claims. Eighteen pages of exhibits were disclosed in judicial review proceedings with the consent of the Foreign and Commonwealth Office. On 27 March 2006 they were passed on to Andrew Tyrie MP at the House of Commons. Two days before the detainees in The Gambia were rendered by the CIA to Afghanistan, and, while they were in American custody, a telegram said on December 6, 2002: 'Further to our telephone conversation, this is to confirm that in relation to Islamists currently in detention in The Gambia, the UK would not seek to extend consular protection to non-British nationals.'[23]

This followed previous telegrams making assertions not subsequently borne out by the facts. There is no evidence, according to Reprieve, that el-Banna was a veteran of the Afghan-Soviet war. The telegram does not back up its assessment that el-Banna was financier to the notorious cleric Abu Qatada. Assessment is not the same as proof.

Bisher al-Rawi is said to have an enthusiasm for 'extreme' sports, as a diver, dinghy sailor and parachutist. He went to Millfield School, in England, which also produced Mary Rand and Duncan Goodhew, both Olympic gold medallists, and Gareth Edwards, who played for Wales and British Lions in the 'extreme' sport of rugby. Al-Rawi had been brought to the attention of the police, having been seen climbing the M4 flyover at Brentford with two companions.

It is not sufficient for MI5 to assert that it did not know beforehand that el-Banna and al-Rawi would be taken to Kabul and then to Guantanamo Bay. The CIA is its ally. They work together in 'the war on terror.' Assurances should have been requested and given. There was no trial before their rendition.

Al-Rawi was released at the end of March 2007. El-Banna then remained in custody. Reprieve said in its news release on 5 April 2007 it was known that in a telegram dated 1 November 2002, the British government tried to present Mr al-Rawi to the US government as an Iraqi Islamist extremist (this memo has been made public in the lawsuit filed on his behalf). Now, the UK government had been forced to concede that, far from being a radical, Mr al-Rawi was quietly helping efforts to combat extremism.

Some of al-Rawi's time in Guantanamo Bay was spent in solitary confinement. This is how 80 per cent of detainees there were being held, according to Amnesty International UK on 5 April 2007.

Amnesty stated:

Guatanamo detainees are held indefinitely as 'enemy combatants', face either no trial at all or an unfair one, have no family visits and no independent expert examinations.

One of the 300 detainees presently held in these conditions is UK resident Shaker Aamer who has been kept in solitary confinement in Camp Echo for more than a year and a half. He is reportedly confined to a small (six-feet by eight-feet) windowless cell with no natural light or fresh air. He is allowed only minimal opportunity for exercise and – apart from a Qu'ran – has no possessions.

Mr Aamer, who has formerly acted as a camp negotiator and may be suffering harsh treatment as a consequence, was at one time denied any exercise outside of his cell for at least 84 consecutive days. He has also reportedly suffered beatings and harassment by camp guards, including having his clothes and mattress removed.'[24]

Can allegations of torture against detainees be substantiated? Stories of torture recur in individual testimonies. Channel 4 Television says that prisoners held in Guantanamo Bay and elsewhere report being ordered to stand motionless for hours at a time. They say they were subjected to extremes of heat and cold, bombarded with bright lights and loud music, and had their sleep patterns interrupted. Detainees report that, in order to demoralise them, they have been insulted and denigrated by religious and racial abuse. Devout Muslims have been humiliated by having to stand naked before others to induce shame and despair. The US government had described 21 attempted suicides at Guantanamo Bay.[25]

The actual role of MI5 in dealing with two men subsequently subject to rendition and detention has to be compared with the emollient-sounding policy enunciated by Eliza Manningham-Buller at the beginning of this chapter and Lord Steyn's comments about possible war crimes.

The MI5 agent who called at el-Banna's home with a Special Branch detective offered him a new life if he would provide details of his activities and contacts. The offer, which would have kept him at large, conflicts with the implication that he was a dangerous Islamist, with the result that he was still locked up after his friend's release.

As I discovered when I refused to spy, MI5 does not like to be turned down. For the first time, there is documentary evidence of MI5's persuasive techniques. It is 'in the 18 pages of exhibits to the open statement of Security Service witness A', disclosed 'in judicial review proceedings'.[26]

An MI5 agent calling himself 'Michael', and 'Andy' of the Special Branch, tried to recruit el-Banna. 'Michael's' note on 31 October 2002 of the meeting gives a rare glimpse of the way MI5 goes about its work and the way in which el-Banna was allowed to believe incorrectly that he was safe to travel to The Gambia, where he was instead seized by the CIA. In my dealings with MI5 argument was used to convince me I should become a spy: I was told that, unless I informed on people, MI5 might get wrong ideas about them and they might suffer. MI5 turned on me later, as this book shows.

The text of notes by the MI5 agent, as placed in the public domain, is given in the following Appendix. Explanations are added in italics.

Appendix

'NOTE FOR FILE

'Date: 31 October 2002

'SUBJECT: Meeting with Abu Anas (*Jamil el-Banna. Abu means 'father of' and Anas is his son's name*).

Summary

'Unannounced visit to ANAS at home by **XXXXX** (*MI5 man*) and MPSB D/Sgt **XXXXX** (*Metropolitan Police Special Branch Detective Sergeant*). ANAS welcoming and apparently friendly, denies any involvement in extremist activity; concerned about being arrested or turned back when leaving for Gambia, or being excluded once outside the country, asks about progress of application for British nationality and possibility of a return of personal items seized during police raid last year, shows no interest in resettlement package in return for co-operation.

'Detail

'2 On 31 October at 0845 hrs, I and XXXXX of MPSB called at ANAS's home. This is a reasonably well-maintained 1930s semi, probably worth around £300,000 if the local estate agents window is anything to go by. Parked on the drive at the front was a small silver-coloured car, VRN ?M439 ELB, displaying a green L plate.

'3 ANAS opened the door himself; in Arabic, I introduced us as Michael from the British Government and Andy from Scotland

Yard and asked if we could have a brief chat with him. He immediately invited us in and took us into the living room at the back of the house; his wife, dressed in traditional full-length hijab, but with the face uncovered, and three young children were already in there so we waited in the corridor in case either ANAS or his wife were sensitive about us being in the same room as her, but they beckoned us in and then said that they were in the middle of checking ANAS's blood sugar level – for the last five days he had been suffering health problems and had just been diagnosed by the doctor as having diabetes. Eventually the wife shooed the children out but hovered around the door to listen to the conversation. The meeting was conducted in Arabic throughout.

'4   ANAS asked me to repeat who we were and I said that I was from the Security Service – Scotland Yard? he queried; so I explained that Andy was from Scotland Yard and that I was from 'the mukhaberaat' (*Arabic for secret police*) although it was important for him to understand that we were not like the mukhaberaat in most Arabic countries. He immediately agreed with this comment.

'5   I then said that, with the arrest of Abu QATADA, we would be able to focus more attention on other members and groups in the extremist community. ANAS immediately said he was not a member of such a group, although he conceded in response to my naming names that he was a friend of Abu QATADA and Abu RASMEE. He explained that as a youth he had led a dissolute life but had then rediscovered Islam and had been to Afghanistan. It was there that he had met QATADA, whom he considered to be a friend; there was no way that he would allow QATADA's family to go without food or assistance during QATADA's detention.

'5   (*The figure 5 is repeated*)   I told him that in addition to increased focus on UK based extremists, we were investigating reports of terrorists based abroad who were keen to mount attacks in the UK, possibly using biological or chemical weapons. He

135

agreed that such people were correctly labelled terrorist. I told him that the use of such techniques would pose a threat to all residents of the UK, as biological weapons would not discriminate between Muslims and Christians, and that as the father of young children he should be concerned by such a possibility. Both ANAS and his wife, who was standing by the door, agreed with this. She then left to look after the children.

'6   I continued saying that in the event of a successful attack in the UK, it was not possible to predict the government's reaction. It was quite possible that he could find himself swept up in a further round of detentions. He did, however, have a choice – he could continue with his current life …; at this point he interrupted to ask what I meant by his current life. He went on to say that he was not involved in any extremist activity, and he did not believe that people like RASMEE could be considered a threat to the UK and, indeed, there was a fatwa which declared that Muslims should respect UK laws. I pointed out that there was also a fatwa which declared that Muslims in the UK could consider themselves to be in a state of jihad and could therefore take 'ghaneema' (spoils of war) from non-Muslims. He … laughed but did not deny this.

'7   He then went on to say that he was not a well man: in addition to diabetes he had trouble with his back due to beatings at the hands of the Jordanian authorities. He was only interested in providing for his children the opportunities he himself had not had as a child. He assumed we knew about his business venture in Gambia with WAHAAB (al-Rawi, brother of Bisher), which he hoped would prove profitable. He said he would be travelling the next day and asked whether he would be arrested or turned back at the airport. I said that if he had a valid travel document he should be able to travel without a problem. He then asked whether he would be able to get back into the country. I repeated the travel document point.

'**8**   I returned to the choice which he could make: he could either continue as at present, with the risks that entailed, or he could start a new life with a new identity, new nationality, money to set himself up in business and to provide for his family, and an opportunity to move to a Muslim country where his children could be brought up away from the bad influences in western society. He asked if I wanted him to leave the UK. I told him that that would be for him to decide but that I could help him if that was what he wanted. He said that his children were being brought up as British nationals, going to normal English schools, his life was now in UK. He then asked about progress on his application for UK nationality as he had completed the required years of residency. I told him that this was a decision for the Home Secretary; he queried whether the Home Secretary decided all cases or only his. I told him that the Home Secretary decided all cases. I added that I was in a position to make recommendations to the Home Secretary but that the final decision rested with the Home Secretary. ANAS asked if the Home Secretary intended to grant his application; I said I did not know but that, if we were asked for a view, we would be obliged to report ANAS's previous involvement in Afghanistan and his association with persons currently detained for extremist activities.

'**9**   I again returned to the choice he had: if he chose to help us by providing details of all his activities and contacts, we would assist him to create a new life for himself and his family. I told him that I did not expect him to give me an immediate answer; it was an important decision and he needed to think carefully about it.

'**10**   ANAS then asked when he could expect the return of the items seized during a police raid on his house some time ago; he explained that his computer, videos, address books had all been taken and not returned. He was particularly keen to get his family photographs back. I told him that I would try to find out what was happening and would let him know.

'11 ANAS's wife had come back in by this time and asked whether we wanted some tea; we declined saying that we were ready to leave. Abu ANAS saw us to the door and waved us off cheerfully.

'Comment

'12 ANAS appeared cheerful and relaxed throughout, although always ready to learn what we knew about him. He maintained that he was not involved in any extremist activity and was focused on his family's welfare. He did not give any hint of willingness to co-operate with us. His desire for British nationality and the security that this would provide may be worth exploring further with him, should he return to the UK. XXXXX will make enquiries of SO13 (*anti-terrorist branch at Scotland Yard*) to establish the status of ANAS's possessions. It may be possible to arrange for the return of some of these items, even in ANAS's absence, to generate some goodwill.

The CIA flew Anas (*Jamil el-Banna*) against his will to Guantanamo Bay after MI5 had put heavy pressure on him, as the note shows, in an attempt to make him an informer. An MI5 agent told him that he and his family would be protected if he agreed. His unforeseen choice turned out to be protection or harsh treatment.

El-Banna described, as a detainee, part of his experience to a tribunal. The text is in document marked 'unclassified'. He said he was 'kidnapped' in The Gambia.

'They took me, covered me, put me in a vehicle and sent me somewhere. I don't know where. It was at night. Then from there to the airport right away.'

Tribunal President: 'An airport in Gambia?'

El-Banna: 'Yes. We were in a room like this with about eight men. All with covered up faces.'

Tribunal President: 'Were you by yourself at that time?'

El-Banna: 'Yes. They cut off my clothes. They were pulling on my hands and my legs.'

Tribunal president: 'When you went to the airport, did you board a plane at that time?'

El-Banna: 'They put me in an airplane and they made me wear the handcuffs that go around your body so I would not do anything on the airplane.'

Tribunal president: 'Okay.'

El-Banna: 'They searched me. They checked my blood. They checked my sugar level. They put me on an airplane – handcuffed me.'

Tribunal president: 'Is this the time you said you were kidnapped?'

El-Banna: 'This is all kidnapping. Yes. They took me underground in the dark. I did not see light for two weeks.'

Tribunal president: 'Is that after you travelled to Afghanistan or Pakistan?'

El-Banna: 'After I got off the airplane.'

Tribunal president: 'In where?'

El-Banna: 'Bagram, Afghanistan. Right there in the dark. They put me in the dark. I was surprised. I did not know what I did wrong or what I did. They starved me; they handcuffed me, there was no food.'

Tribunal president: 'And they are who?'

El-Banna: 'Americans. I was under their control. They are the ones who took me and they put me there. They know what they have done. I was surprised that the Americans would do such a thing. It shocked me.'

It will be argued that Islamist militants must be persuaded to co-operate by providing information. The bombing of London happened because MI5 was given no forewarning. The whole direction since has been to toughen a response which has hit not only the Islamist extremists but the rest of the population as well and allowed the executive generally to gain coercive power in its bid to prevent further terrorist attacks.

On the basis of the documented evidence and Lord Steyn's comments the question is whether there is a *prima facie* case for a charge against Britain of war crimes, subject to proof and the understanding that the kind of treatment meted out to Mr el-Banna and others amounts to torture. Torture need not be physical but can be mental, which must surely be enhanced by any miscarriage, or absence, of justice.

Misjudgements are dangerous when lives are at stake, whether those of individuals or of thousands at risk from bombing, as the next chapter will show.[27]

10

The London Bombers Free to Kill

The bombs that killed 52 people in London on 7 July 2005 were made by young Muslim terrorists in a modern block of flats in Leeds. The ingredients were readily for sale commercially. So strong were the fumes that the windows had to be opened to enable the men to work, and the tops of plants just outside died from the effects. Two of the men, at least, bought face masks. Their hair became noticeably lighter, which they blamed on chlorine in swimming pools.

According to the official account of the London bombings,[1] the first purchase of the bomb-making material was on 31 March 2005. On 28 June a dummy run is thought to have been made by three of the terrorists, Shehzad Tanweer, Mohammad Sidique Khan and Jermaine Lindsay, but not by their fellow terrorist, Hasib Hussain. Lindsay was later found to have charted times between train stations.

Before dawn on 7 July they began their countdown to murder. Their light blue Nissan Micra, hired by Tanweer, was picked up on CCTV at 3.58 a.m. near to the bomb factory, which was next to the Leeds Grand Mosque, before joining the M1. The Micra stopped at Woodall service station at 4.54 am for petrol. Tanweer paid for it, bought snacks and quibbled with the cashier over his change. He was wearing a white T-shirt, dark jacket, white tracksuit bottoms and a baseball cap.

Jermaine Lindsay drove alone in a red Fiat Brava to Luton station and parked at 5.07 a.m. The Micra parked next to it at 6.49 am.

141

The four got out and put on large, fully packed rucksacks, each containing an estimated 2-5 kg of high explosive. A 9mm handgun was later found in one of the cars and a different and smaller variety of explosive devices.

The official account of the day says a CCTV camera caught the four at 7.21 a.m. going to the platform for the King's Cross train leaving at 7.40 am. There was nothing exceptional about them which would have aroused suspicion. Arriving at King's Cross at 8.23 a.m. the four were seen hugging and looking happy, even euphoric. They walked towards the targeted trains.

CCTV, this time at Liverpool Street, showed the eastbound Circle Line train seconds before it was blown up and smoke billowed from the tunnel. Forensic evidence suggested that Tanweer was sitting towards the back of the second carriage with the rucksack next to him on the floor. He was among 8 people to die, with 171 injured.

Likewise, Mohammed Sidique Khan was in the second carriage from the front of the train at Edgware Road. He was one of 7 killed. Another 163 were injured.

Lindsay was probably standing in the first carriage of a Piccadilly Line train between King's Cross and Russell Square when his bomb exploded. He was among 27 people killed and more than 340 injured.

Hussain was the exception. At 8.55 a.m. he walked out of King's Cross underground station to Euston Road before going to W.H. Smith's on the station concourse, apparently to buy a 9v battery, possibly needed to detonate his bomb. At 9.06 a.m. he went into McDonalds on Euston Road for ten minutes. It is believed that at Euston he switched from one bus to another – the No 30 from Marble Arch. Someone of his description was seen fiddling repeatedly with his rucksack, leading to speculation that the new battery was needed to replace a faulty one, thus preventing synchronisation with the other explosions. He detonated his bomb at 9.47 a.m. and died with 13 others. More than 110 were injured.

The explosions took MI5 by surprise. Intelligence experts had previously downgraded the terrorist threat from 'severe general', the second highest level, to the lower category of 'substantial'. That was lower than it had been since the United States was attacked on September 11, 2001. In London 56 people, including the bombers, died, and more than 700 were injured.

The altered threat level was the more pointed because of the timing. Enormous security measures had been taken to safeguard world leaders at the G8 summit in Scotland. And there was euphoria over the decision to have the Olympic games in Britain. The official view is that the timing was fortuitous, but it was a perfect occasion for a devastating blow to be struck against the West. A security risk was appreciated in Scotland by the authorities, but not in relation to London. The failure was to concentrate on it in Scotland at the expense of cover elsewhere – a classic case of wrong-footing. Officers in charge of security at the conference said after the attack that many of the 1,500 Metropolitan police deployed there would be urgently returned to London.

The downgrading of the terrorist threat was compounded by an up-beat assessment on 7 July by Sir Ian Blair, Metropolitan Police Commissioner, just before the attacks. Speaking on BBC's Radio 4 at 7.20 a.m., he said: 'We have been described by Her Majesty's Inspectorate of Constabulary as the envy of the policing world in relation to counter-terrorism, and I am absolutely positive that our ability is there.'

He said about a potential threat: 'It is difficult to calculate whether it is inevitable that they will get through.' They did. At 7.21 a.m. the four terrorists were pictured at Luton railway station on closed circuit television on their way to London to detonate their bombs.

There were immediate denials from MI5 that it was in any way at fault. Security sources were quoted in *The Times* next day[2] as saying it was realised that there would be accusations that the intelligence services had failed. 'But we have always warned that intelligence never reveals a complete picture. It's a cheap shot to blame the intelligence services; but nothing was known in advance of these attacks,' an official said.

143

Antony Barnett and Martin Bright told a different story in the *Observer* of 2 October 2005.[3] They wrote that ministers, senior police officers and top civil servants were shocked at MI5's lack of intelligence after the 7 July terrorist attacks. Their senior Whitehall source was at meetings of Cobra, the Government's crisis command group convened to react to the London bombings.

The Whitehall official who attended the emergency meetings told the *Observer* there was general shock at the absence of information coming from the intelligence services about who was behind the London bombings. 'We were all waiting for some answers. We lived in hope that the security service would provide a thread or a sliver, but no. That was a shock to the system.'[4]

Using information in the official account, we will examine what in the lives of the four bombers turned them into killers and whether MI5 should have been alerted to the danger they posed.

Khan, aged 30 at the time of the outrage, was the oldest of the group and apparent ringleader. Like Tanweer (aged 22 when he died) and Hussein (who was 18) they were second generation British citizens of Pakistani immigrants to Yorkshire. All three grew up on the outskirts of Leeds and were educated locally. Khan gained a 2.2 in business studies at Leeds Metropolitan University, where he discovered a vocation for helping disadvantaged young people and met his future wife, a British Muslim of Indian origin. He worked at a local primary school, where he was highly regarded by parents and teachers, calming difficult children and guiding those with special needs.

Tanweer was also talented academically and at sport, particularly at cricket and athletics. He studied sports science at Leeds Metropolitan University up to BSc level, but he had no paid work after a spell helping in his father's fish and chip shop. His father wanted to set him up in business.

Hussein was less of an achiever, but finished a college course in advanced business studies.

Lindsay was different. His mother was 19 when he was born in Jamaica in 1985. His father stayed there when she left for Huddersfield

with another man. Lindsay gained a second step-father as the result
of a new relationship, with whom he was closer. Artistic and
musical, he was good academically and at sport, with a teenage
interest in martial arts and kick-boxing.

Apart from Lindsay's disrupted background – and that is not
decisive – there was nothing at this stage in their behaviour to
indicate why any of the four might turn into anything other than
socially conforming members of society.

Khan prayed regularly at work and in the Mosque on Fridays.
An incident in a nightclub is said to have changed his life and
turned him to religion, but not fanatically so, at least in the way
he talked about it. At work he spoke out against the attacks in
America on 9/11. He was dismissed from the school where he
worked after taking sick leave, regarded as unjustified, at the end
of 2004.

Tanweer, religious when quite young, became more so when 17,
and, after leaving university early, appeared to spend most of his
time studying the Prophet's teachings and observing them. He went
to a religious school at Dewsbury. But he owned a red Mercedes
given him by his father, had his hair styled and wore designer
clothes.

Hussain, large in build and quiet at school, became more intensely
religious after a Haj visit to Saudi Arabia with his family in 2002.
He turned to traditional clothing – white on Fridays – and a prayer
cap. Openly in support of al-Qaeda at school, he said the 9/11
bombers were martyrs and wrote in his RE schoolbook: 'Al Qaeda
no limits'. He told a teacher he wished to become a cleric. He
read religious texts and prayed into the early hours.

The group attended three local mosques and others elsewhere.
Khan emerged as a leading figure when he, Tanweer and Hussain
got to know each other socially. The official account suggests Khan
observed life going on around a gymnasium and Islamic bookshop
to see who could later be indoctrinated – privately to avoid detection.

Part of Khan's programme was to arrange camping, canoeing,
white water rafting and other outward-bound style adventures. These

activities, in which physical fitness was a must, are not called 'training' in the official account, but any serviceman would recognise them as such, as a means of encouraging bonding and discipline, along with the testing of one's mettle. Another reason why these activities were more than merely recreational is that they were attended not only by the 7 July bombers but also by other cells disrupted before and since. As we know, Khan's group was left unchallenged.

Like the others, Lindsay, the outsider, was physically fit and regularly worked out. He followed his mother's conversion to Islam in 2000 and took the name Jamal. He was disciplined at school for handing out leaflets in support of al-Qaeda. Lindsay quickly became fluent in Arabic and wore the traditional white robe. The preacher, Abdallah al Faisal, is believed to have influenced him strongly when Lindsay attended at least one lecture and listened to tapes of others. (The facts are from the report of the official account of the London bombings.)

MI5's fundamental mistake, from which others flowed, was its failure to appreciate a link with Pakistan, a known source of terrorism. Khan and Tanweer went there from 19 November 2004 to 8 February 2005, and the report speculates that the visit may have been 'an important element' in deciding to mount a bombing attack. 'Who they may have met in Pakistan has not yet been established, but it seems likely that they had some contact with al-Qaeda figures.' The report believes Khan received relevant training in a remote part of Pakistan during a two-week visit in July 2003. He may earlier have been to Afghanistan.

The official account adds that, between April and July 2005, the group was in contact with an individual or individuals in Pakistan. It is not known who this was or the content of the contacts but the methods used, designed to make it difficult to identify the individual, make the contacts look suspicious.

The extent of the terrorists' preparations is further disclosed in the report of the Intelligence and Security Committee into the bombings. Investigations have shown that the group was in contact with others involved in extremism in the UK. 'The extent to which the July 7 attacks were externally planned, directed or controlled by contacts in Pakistan or elsewhere remains unclear.' Contacts in the run-up to the attacks suggested that they might have had advice or direction from individuals there.

The evidence to the Committee makes plain – although it is not explicit in saying so – that MI5 and its associates missed all the clues of importance that were left in their path. 'We have been told in evidence that none of the individuals involved in the 7 July Group had been identified (that is, named and listed) as potential terrorist threats prior to July. We have also been told that there was no warning from intelligence (including foreign intelligence) of the plans to attack the London Transport network on 7 July.'[5]

Once the bombs had gone off, MI5 found it had come across Sidique Khan and Shazad Tanweer before. It identified a telephone number in its files as that of Jermaine Lindsay. Also in its records was another number registered to 'Sidique Khan' and details of contacts between it and another person who had been under investigation in 2003. 'A review of related surveillance data showed that Khan and Tanweer had been among a group of men who had held meetings with others under Security Service investigation in 2004.' The word 'held' implies the meetings were more than casual. According to the Security Service there was no reason for Khan to have been identified as exceptional or worthy of further investigation above other priorities.

Khan and Tanweer were regarded as peripheral to 'an important and substantial on-going investigation'. The Security Service 'did not seek to investigate or identify them at the time although it would probably have been possible to do so had the decision been taken'. There was no intelligence to suggest they were planning an attack on the UK.

However, evidence to the Committee makes it clear that Khan and Tanweer were known then. 'Intelligence at the time suggested that their focus was training and insurgency operations in Pakistan, and schemes to defraud financial institutions.'

Further details of Khan's visit were disclosed by CBS News on August 18 2005: 'A source familiar with the investigation has told CBS news that an American al-Qaeda operative, now in US custody, told the FBI that he escorted Sidique Khan to a terrorist training camp in Northern Pakistan.' The operative told the FBI that another group of alleged British terrorists was in Pakistan at the time. CBS News said: 'For days after the bombing, British officials insisted the cell had been flying beneath their radar. It now appears at least one of the bombers crossed their sights, but they failed to understand what they were looking at.'[6]

There was evidently a failure to see information about Pakistan in relation to facts obtained from MI5's 'important and substantial ongoing investigation', and then for the investigation to switch tack. That would presumably not have needed new resources but the redeployment of those MI5 already had. The 7 July attack on London was the biggest threat of all.

MI5 failed to identify Khan as a visitor to Pakistan in 2003. Yet a detainee from outside the UK spoke of men from Britain, known only by pseudonyms, who had sought meetings with al-Qaeda figures.

The Committee's report says: 'The fact that there were suicide attacks in the UK on 7 July was clearly unexpected: the Director General of the Security Service (Eliza Manningham-Buller) said it was a surprise that the first big attack in the UK for 10 years was a suicide attack.[7] ... We are concerned that this judgement could have had an impact on the alertness of the authorities to the kind of threat they were facing and their ability to respond.' Nor was the threat of home-grown terrorism fully understood or countered.

Through no fault of its own, the Committee's opinions were seriously flawed, according to later revelations. A political row followed exposure of an alleged cover-up by MI5 of crucial evidence.[8] Accusations of a 'whitewash' came from politicians and victims of the attacks. MI5 was alleged to have failed to reveal to the committee that it bugged the leader of the 7 July suicide bombers discussing the building of a bomb months before the London attacks.

The existence of tape recordings of one of the bombers was disclosed by David Davis, Shadow Home Secretary, in the House of Commons. He is reported in *The Sunday Times* as telling John Reid, the Home Secretary:

It seems that MI5 taped Mohammad Sidique Khan talking about his wish to fight in the jihad and saying his goodbyes to his family – a clear indication that he was intending a suicide mission ... he was known to have attended late-stage discussions on planning another major terror attack. Again, I ask the Home Secretary whether that is true.[9]

Mr Reid said the questions were legitimate but failed to answer them.

I wrote to the secretary of the Committee on 16 May 2006:

As the authority of the committee would be involved, I would ask, please, what it is doing, firstly, to check the allegations; secondly, how it would disclose its findings; and, thirdly, what it would do if it had deliberately been denied information vital to national security. Since yours is a statutory committee, and not a select committee, I am wondering if contempt might be an issue.

Questions are raised, also, of course, about the accountability of MI5, as they have been in the past.[10]

The letter requested any information on the matter.

Paul Murphy MP, chairman, later denied that the Security Service withheld any evidence from the committee.[11] However, the number of discrepancies between facts obtained by experienced reporters from sources at the time and reassuring quotes later from establishment figures enhanced, rather than diminished, the need for an independent inquiry.

MI5's alibi – it uses alibis skilfully – for the failure to pre-empt the bombings of London on 7 July was a shortage of money which, it claimed, prevented leads being investigated. The evidence shows this to be incorrect and an excuse for poor targeting. Criticism began to mount. Its timing as good as ever, MI5 released an eye-catching total of terror suspects for publication in the *Observer* on 14 May 2006.[12] The more MI5 looked, the more 'suspects' it found. The newspaper said: 'The number of Islamist terror suspects in Britain being targeted by the security service, MI5, has soared to 1,200, a 50 per cent rise since the London suicide bombings last July.' And 20 serious terrorist plots have been found (*The Sunday Times* 28 May 2006) so, according to MI5, time could not be spared for a feared inquiry, which could scrutinise its claims.

Given its alleged shortage of money, how did MI5 know what the increase actually was in numbers of 'terror suspects'? The only sure way of finding out was to investigate each suspect's status. Otherwise, the result is hearsay or a guess. If MI5 could target 1,200 and judge them all to be suspects – seemingly potential terrorists – why could it not target the mere four who turned out to be lethal bombers on 7 July? MI5 is inconsistent. Where did all these suspects come from so suddenly? Were they to be dealt with via anti-terror laws or were they not a threat? Such startling claims will not, of course, receive independent verification.

MI5's complaints of money shortages conflict with facts from the Treasury. The security services received all the resources they had asked for in the 2004 spending review (BBC News, 5 May 2006).

MI5 brought some of its alleged troubles on itself by taking work from the police. In 1996, when dangerous Islamist militancy was in the ascendant. MI5 spent precious resources on a new extra role for itself – the investigation of serious crime. This is disclosed in its own official handbook.[13] MI5 received no additional money for its new role. So crime fighting was at the expense of its other work.

Yet there was firm evidence of the growing terrorist menace. Explosives were used in 1992 against hotels in Somalia where US troops were staying. The following year the World Trade Center experienced its first attack. And 1995 saw the start of a four-month campaign in France by the Armed Islamic Group (GIA). As MI5 began encroaching on police territory in pursuit of criminals, a truck bomb, in June 1996, went off in a housing complex in Saudi Arabia. Ominously, Osama bin Laden published his *fatwa*: 'Declaration of War against the Americans occupying the Land of the Two Holy Places (Saudi Arabia).' That was in August, 1996, just two months after MI5 began chasing criminals. Militants were becoming active in Britain.

Melanie Phillips in her book *Londonistan*[14] describes how in the 1980s and 1990s Islamist radicals flocked to London. Her extracts in the *Daily Mail* of 20 May 2006 record how London fostered the growth of myriad radical Islamist publications and preachers spitting hatred of the west. 'Its banks were used for fund-raising accounts funnelling money into extremist and terrorist organisations, and it provided the launching pad for many of Osama Bin Laden's *fatwas*.' Terrorists wanted in other countries were given safe haven in the UK. But where was MI5?

More recent evidence of MI5's misguided expansion into new territory is a decision, without any apparent objection, to give it primacy over the police in Northern Ireland against the Real IRA and Continuity IRA – not so onerous a task as the police have faced there in the past. It is odd that, like the police in Britain, those in Northern Ireland are not given sufficient credit for the talent they possess. The decision to hand over control was taken in February 2005 – before the bombings. The result is that figures available in 2006 showed that 21 per cent of MI5's budget was being devoted to countering Irish terrorism. That will not be needed now and can surely be transferred to operations against Islamist terrorism. Presumably the anti-terror police might get a fairer share of Government financing.

MI5's priorities are questioned in a report by the prestigious think tank Chatham House and the Economic & Social Research Council (ESRC).[15] The report, based on a five-year research project, said on 18 July 2005 that an understandable preoccupation with terrorism related to Northern Ireland diverted the attention of Britain's intelligence agencies away from international terrorism. As a result the security services failed to give priority in the early 1990s to monitoring Islamic terror activists setting up in Britain. The British authorities did not fully appreciate the threat from al-Qaeda.

Not only was there the attack, with fatalities, on 7 July 2005, but on 21 July there were four incidents in London, between 12.35 and 13.05, on underground trains and a bus. Again no warning was given. The speed with which police acted showed their efficiency when required, although the fatal shooting of a Brazilian, Charles de Menezes, mistaken for a suicide bomber, detracted from Scotland Yard's wider achievement.

The police and customs were already fighting serious crime when MI5 began involving itself. MI5's proposed new role had been criticised by Lord Jenkins of Hillhead (Roy Jenkins), former Home Secretary. No-one was in a better position to do so than he. Jenkins said in the House of Lords on 19 December 1993:

'I am not convinced that the international crime rings are a suitable new target for the security services. I believe that the police are much more skilled and expert in dealing with crime than are the security services.'[16]

BBC News reported on 11 May 2006 that at one stage before the September 11 attacks in America, serious crime took up about 15 per cent of MI5's resources. Its work against drug trafficking and large-scale fraud has been handed over to the new Serious Organised Crime Agency, under yet another man from MI5, Sir Stephen Lander, who had previously headed it.

MI5's claims about shortage of money are further undermined. Subversion, once a drain on resources, is no longer so, and money has been saved for use elsewhere. Extra funds were already flowing to MI5 for its anti-terrorist work. This is noted in the annual report (2004–5) of the Intelligence and Security Committee.

Shortage of money is not MI5's only excuse. Part of its alibi for failure before the London bombings is that no information of importance came in. Journalists who also have to get facts do not wait for something to come in; they go out and find it, or they may lose their jobs. They have contacts where it matters, and penetrate trouble-spots. MI5 failed to find out what Mohammed Sidique Khan was up to in Pakistan with, presumably the host country's secret intelligence service willing to help. Yet one *Daily Mail* reporter, David Williams, was able to write later from Rawalpindi (on 8 May 2006) exactly what Sidique Khan and Tanweer had been doing.[17] That was before the official report came out. Sidique Khan was taught how to make weapons and use arms. Williams, of course, did not have the aid of GCHQ and phone tapping.

Peculiarly, the police get too little recognition in the official reports of the bombings. Due credit is not given to them for their work against terrorism.

Sidique Khan was not the only terrorist MI5 allowed to slip through its fingers. Neil Mackay, the home affairs editor of the *Sunday Herald*, reported on 30 September 2001[18] that at least 11 members of the hijack teams that hit America on 9/11 had been in Britain and none of them had been under surveillance by British intelligence during their time here. British spy-masters were completely in the dark about the activities of the hijackers until the FBI alerted them.

Mackay wrote that Bin Laden's al-Qaeda organisation openly operated in London for most of the 1990s under the name of the Advisory and Reformation Committee. He corroborates Melanie Phillips's account of 'Londonistan' by saying that a handful of ultra-violent Islamic groups was able to operate from Britain with relative impunity.

Other terrorists fell through the net. The *Observer* had earlier disclosed, on 30 December 2001,[19] that British intelligence knew of links between the shoe bomber, Richard Reid, and one 9/11 hijack suspect but failed to track Reid before he tried to blow up an airliner. The *Observer* was citing US intelligence reports. Scotland Yard was apparently not informed of the security risk Reid posed.

The muted findings of the Intelligence and Security Committee contrast with the frankness, criticism and willingness to blame which the US investigations displayed following the 9/11 attacks. The British findings were unlikely to bring about similar fundamental change.

The bombings imply a need for a re-appraisal of MI5's nature, role, aspirations and competence. But there has been no adequate independent inquiry, nothing open and really searching. The excuse in Britain was that such an inquiry would disrupt intelligence work. That would have carried no weight in the United States where vigorous investigations stirred the nation.

George Tenet, director of the CIA, resigned – for personal reasons, he said. The CIA was at the centre of criticism for intelligence failures before the Iraq war and then for the 9/11 outrages. There were suggestions that the US should have an agency like MI5, but, significantly, that was rejected on civil liberties grounds.

Michael Howard's call, as Conservative leader, on 11 July 2005 for a full inquiry into possible security failures in Britain before the London bombings was rejected by Downing Street. An official said that Tony Blair had absolute confidence in the security services and police. Further calls for an inquiry followed the leak and eventual publication of the Intelligence and Security Committee's report into the London bombings.

The cover-up in Britain contrasts with the frank criticism in the United States of the CIA leadership over failures before the attacks on September 11, 2001. An inquiry by the CIA openly blamed George Tenet, its former director for the failures.[20] An internal report was completed in June 2005 and declassified on 21 August 2007. It said top officers in the CIA 'did not discharge their responsibilities in a satisfactory manner'. There was 'systematic breakdown' in a watch list for tracking terrorism suspects who seek to enter the United States (*The Times* 22 August 2007).

So was there a systematic breakdown, with MI5 and MI6 to blame, in a similar watch list in Britain? The evidence is in the next chapter.

Some of the Government's touchiness is because the London bombings on 7 July were part of a wider, scandalous intelligence failure which had much earlier become apparent before the Falklands War in 1982, when Argentina's invasion was not as urgently anticipated as might have been wished. More recently a dependence on faulty information used by the United States and Britain has cast doubts on the motives for going to war against Iraq. Colin Powell who, as US Secretary of State, told the United Nations that Saddam Hussein was hiding weapons of mass destruction, now regrets his assertion. He blames the mistake on failure within the intelligence community to acknowledge that sources could not be relied upon.[21]

Probably the frankest confession in Britain of error over Iraq's weapons of mass destruction (WMD) came from the Joint Intelligence Committee. In December 2004, it reviewed judgement on the WMD capability and programmes some of which formed the basis of the September 2002 dossier:

Nuclear weapons (2002): *'Iraq is pursuing a nuclear weapons programme. But it will not be able to indigenously produce a nuclear weapon while sanctions remain in place.'*

The truth: The JIC judgement was wrong in that Iraq was not pursuing a nuclear weapons programme; but it was right on Iraq's nuclear ambitions and its inability to produce a nuclear weapon under sanctions.

Ballistic weapons (2002): *'Iraq retains up to 20 Al-Hussein ballistic missiles.'*

The truth: The claim has not been substantiated.

Chemical weapons (2002): *'Iraq may retain some stocks of chemical agents ... Iraq could produce significant quantities of mustard within weeks, significant quantities of Sarin and VX (nerve gas) within months and in the case of VX may already have done so.'*

The truth: Although a capability to produce some agents probably existed, this judgement has not been substantiated.

Biological weapons (2002): *'Iraq currently has available, either from pre (before the) Gulf War, or more recent production, a number of biological agents ... Iraq could produce more of these biological agents within days.'*

The truth: The Iraq Survey Group found that Iraq had dual-use facilities which could have allowed production of biological weapons to resume but not within the time-frames judged by the Joint Intelligence Committee, and found no evidence that production had been activated. [The Iraq Survey Group was sent by the multinational force after the invasion to find any weapons of mass destruction developed by Saddam Hussein.][22]

This analysis by the JIC is published in the annual report of the Intelligence and Security Committee for 2004–5. So Britain went to war in Iraq, and the credibility of intelligence evaporated – just as it had a generation earlier over failure to predict that Argentina was about to invade the Falklands.

The Intelligence and Security Committee is not noted for its harsh and sweeping criticisms. It concludes:

While this report includes a number of criticisms and concerns relating to the UK intelligence community, we would not wish these points to overshadow the essential and excellent work that the agencies have undertaken. As ever, much of this work will never be reported and therefore we wish to place on record our appreciation of the staff within the UK intelligence community. Without their work, the UK would not have been protected against terrorist attack.

But it wasn't. Even as the report was being presented to Parliament by the Prime Minister in April 2005, the terrorists were preparing

11

'Not the Whole Truth': MI5's Alibi

MI5's failure to dispel allegations of a cover-up over the London bombings led to angry demands for an independent inquiry. It came from victims of the bomb outrage and opposition front-benchers who pressed for the full truth to be told.

Their protests followed evidence that MI5 had secretly monitored two of the London suicide bombers on four occasions a year before the attacks in 2005.[1] The extent to which MI5 knew about Mohammed Sidique Khan and Shehzad Tanweer emerged after the trial of conspirators in another terrorist plot which had been foiled. Khan was surreptitiously recorded discussing terrorism with the plotters' leader.[2] He was not investigated further.[3] Yet MI5 knew his name, address, car number and telephone number 16 months before the 7 July bombing.[4] The refusal of Tony Blair to agree to an investigation reflected MI5's dark power to influence government and avoid scrutiny.

For legal reasons, known details of links with the London suicide bombers, Mohammad Sidique Khan and Shezad Tanweer, had to await publication until after the trial. Five British Muslims were given life sentences for plotting a massive UK attack with fertiliser bomb blast techniques.[5] The intended targets included a shopping centre or night club. All five convicted men had attended terror training camps in Pakistan.[6] They later sought leave to appeal (see note at end of the chapter).

Four times police and MI5 agents had seen the two suicide

159

bombers, later to commit mass murder, meeting some of the plotters in 2004. The leading fertiliser bomb conspirator, Omar Khyam, not only met Khan four times in this country but once more in Pakistan.[7] Khyam also met Tanweer three times, according to information placed before the court.

Four times Khan and Tanweer were photographed with the plotters.[8] Khan first came to the notice of intelligence chiefs in 2003. They are reckoned to have missed 12 chances to arrest the 7/7 cell between then and the day when 52 people died in the London bombings. Both MI5 and the Metropolitan Police insisted that they had no reason to think Khan and Tanweer were dangerous. They dismissed them as credit-card fraudsters raising money to aid militants abroad.

Fresh doubts about the extent of knowledge by MI5 about the London suicide bombers emerged from a 37-page document prepared for the Crown Prosecution Service.[9] It states that Khan was 'identified' six months before the attacks in which 52 people died. The CPS document, reportedly cleared by MI5's legal department, says that MI5 surveillance showed that Khan and Tanweer 'were concerned with intended terrorist activity' when they met with the fertiliser bomb plotters. John Reid. Home Secretary, had told MPs that neither of the pair was known to MI5 until after the bombing.

Khan and Tanweer turned out to be part of activity connecting British born extremists to a skein from North America to Pakistan, linked by intelligence to al-Qaeda.[10]

Outraged victims of the atrocity called for an independent inquiry. Rachel North, who survived the bomb on the Piccadilly Line train, said she was 'shocked and appalled' to hear that Khan was a close associate of Omar Khyam, one of the convicted plotters. She had believed government and security officials who had said nothing was known about those involved or could have been done to prevent the bombing. The shattering of that illusion came as a massive shock. Charles Clarke (then Home Secretary) had said: 'These bombings came out of the blue, these men are clean skins.'[11]

Rachel North added:

It was tempting to believe that these guys had never been known to the police or the security services, that they had somehow managed to make these bombs and drive down to London and get on tube trains and a bus and that it was a terrible tragedy and there was nothing anybody could have done to stop them.

When it transpired that was not the case it was devastating. This has fuelled my desire for an independent inquiry because it appears we have not been told the truth about what happened and what we knew about these bombers prior to 7/7.[12]

She believed the disclosures meant the atrocity could have been prevented.

In refusing an inquiry Tony Blair did not wish to undermine MI5's confidence. But the problem is not its under-confidence but its over-confidence, which leads it into misjudgements, as this book clearly shows. The Intelligence and Security Committee failed initially to see all it should have done. Mr Blair's reaction poses the question of what he had to fear. His refusal of an inquiry protected State power at the expense of distraught victims.

Mr Blair said that the committee was the right body to examine intelligence handling. He stated: 'If we now say, effectively, that the Intelligence and Security Committee inquiry was not adequate, and if we hold another inquiry ... we shall not get any more truth because the truth is there in the Intelligence and Security Committee. What we shall do is undermine support for our security services, and I am simply not prepared to do that.'[13]

His statement prompted more questions than it answered. How could MI5's support be undermined by the truth? Was not its support already being undermined by failure to convince sceptical critics that it was blameless? Why should great anxiety and difficulty be caused within the service, if an inquiry found all was well with it? If it did not, then reform, better control and discipline needed to be imposed to protect the lives of British people from atrocities. As it stood, Mr Blair's statement simply implied a loss of faith in

MI5 because its position was too fragile to be examined.

Opposition frontbenchers responded sharply to Ministers' stonewalling:

- Sir Menzies Campbell, Liberal democrat leader: 'The information revealed in this trial will spark widespread public concern and debate about the operational capabilities of the security service, and the reliability of government information in the aftermath of the July 7 bombings.'
- David Davis, Shadow Home Secretary said that a decision to rebut the allegations on a website was not the answer. 'Whether deliberately or not, the Government has not told the British public the whole truth about the circumstances and mistakes leading up to the July 7 attacks...[14]

The case produced a barrage of media revelations. They included a transcript of a conversation bugged by MI5 between Omar Khyam, the jailed ringleader of the fertiliser bomb plot, and Mohammad Sidique Khan, the London suicide bomber. BBC News (1 May 2007), which published the transcript, said officers recorded Khan in Khyam's car on 21 February 2004.

Khyam is reported as asking:

This is a one-way ticket, bruv, and you agree with that, yeah? You're happy with this and em, er, basically (unclear) because you're going to leave now, you may as well rip the country apart economically as well. All the brothers are running scams, and I advise you to do the same... All the brothers that (are) leaving are doing it... Now that's all I've got to say, bruv. Is there anything you'd like to ask? Then fire away.

The text, as disclosed, requires further examination, for it says: 'You may as well rip the country apart economically *as well*.' The italics are mine. As a journalist I would at that point have wished to ask him: 'As well as what?' Certainly it is as well as something.

When this is put alongside a later quote of Mohammad Sidique Khan talking about his child, there appears to be added meaning: 'With regards to the babe, I'm debating whether or not to say goodbye and so forth.' 'Goodbye' sounds ominously final.

> Khan asks Khyam: 'Are you really a terrorist, eh?
> Khyam: 'They're working with us.'
> Khan: 'You're serious. You are basically.'
> Khyam: 'No, I'm not a terrorist but they are working through us.'
> Khan: 'Who are, there's no-one higher than you (unclear).'

The question is, did MI5 officers evaluate the conversation by themselves, or did they bring in police who, in enforcing the law, know about conspiracies or, at a lower level, simply about aiding and abetting?

The most intriguing revelation came in the *Guardian* of 3 May 2007,[15] that Tanweer was surfing the internet for bomb-making tips in June 2005, two weeks before the suicide attacks. He was heard to be discussing bombings and using the internet to make such a bomb, according to a document which prosecution lawyers in the fertiliser bomb plot case disclosed to the defence before the trial began. The document said: 'Tanweer told the same person he had entered Afghanistan and met people from around the world who had got into his head.'

The *Guardian* quoted MI5 as saying the information was 'false'. However, the Crown Prosecution Service told the *Guardian* the information was passed to it by Scotland Yard.[16] The Yard did not deny that, but said its officers in the case had 'no recollection' of the information. The sequence of events provides cumulative evidence that was ignored. Sidique Khan remained unidentified as a potential threat.

Yet the *Guardian* reported on 1 May 2007 that Sidique Khan saw terrorist suspects on 2 February 2004, and then was photographed at Toddington Service Station on the M1 driving a green Honda

163

Civic. His wife was the registered owner. Later that month, MI5 tailed Khan and Tanweer in the green Honda for 15 hours. They were in a two-car convoy with Khyam in another vehicle. Khyam, followed by Khan and Tamweer, was in turn followed by MI5 on 23 March 2004, as they drove from Crawley to Slough, then to Upton Park, London, and back to Slough.

Even after Khyam and his fellow plotters were rounded up the re-registration of the Civic in Khan's name still did not alert MI5. Even now MI5 was unable to identify the man who was to go on to lead the 7 July bombers.

The Intelligence and Security Committee examined the events surrounding the London bombings, as we have seen in the previous chapter. The ISC report in 2006 said: 'We have been told in evidence that none of the ... 7 July group has been identified (that is named and listed) as potential terrorist threats prior to July.'[18]

The committee's chairman, Paul Murphy MP, told the BBC on 30 April 2007 that he stood by the committee's findings. He said on Newsnight that MI5 had not identified Khan until after he died.[19] John Reid, Home Secretary, asked the Committee to reappraise its report on the bombings. But Paul Murphy said that the fresh disclosures did not change his view that there had been 'no culpable failures by the security and intelligence agencies'.[20]

MI5 explained on its website:

Khan and Tanweer were never identified during the fertiliser plot investigation because they were not involved in the planned attacks. Rather they appeared as petty fraudsters in loose contact with members of the plot. There was no indication that they were involved in planning any kind of terrorist attack in the UK.[21]

MI5 has denied failing to pass on to West Yorkshire police the result of its surveillance of Khan. A police examination would have established more about him, which might have stimulated further inquiries and established him as a threat – something MI5 did not do. Even if the police did receive the evidence, that hardly excuses

MI5, glad to be in the lead in security matters, if it did not check to see what was discovered or failed to pursue its own leads.

The police evidently followed up, on their own initiative, a lead on Khan only five months before the London bombing. They took a statement from a garage manager in Leeds who had loaned him a courtesy car previously followed by MI5. The garage manager told police that the car had been loaned to a Mr S. Khan, who gave his mobile telephone number and an address in Batley, West Yorkshire.[22]

The relationship between the police and MI5 has been explored in earlier chapters. If the police took a statement from the garage owner, they obviously meant business, although many other statements were also made. MI5 has reportedly said that inquiries into Khan ended in 2004 (*Guardian*, 3 May 2007). As we have earlier seen, police initiative is increasingly being frustrated by the bureaucracy. The question is whether the police, if left alone and safely passed information by MI5, would have been able to act more decisively against the London bombers. The feeling remains that Special Branch, which came into being to fight terrorism, might have been better placed to take the lead than MI5. Adequate follow-up is always vital.

In giving information after the London bombing MI5 was either incompetent or misleading. Journalists were told that Khan and his other bombers were 'clean skins', jargon meaning that nothing was known of any previous terrorist connections.[23]

Much praise has rightly been heaped on MI5 and the police for the way they rounded up the fertiliser bomb conspirators. MI5 technicians are good at their job: bugging and, with the aid of GCHQ, telephone tapping, or computer penetration. Their bosses' judgement is not so impressive, however. And if they wished to prioritise, where was I in the list, with my telephone tapped and other surveillance of me being carried out? I had been told that I was a target, as previous chapters have described. That was a waste of resources, which might have been better spent on Sidique Khan.

MI5 would not have deserved such acclaim, however, without two crucial outside interventions.

Electronic eavesdropping by America's National Security Agency

(NSA) picked up traffic between Britain and Pakistan which suggested a potential terrorist attack. The message appeared to come from al-Qaeda sources. Police and MI5 mustered forces. A massive anti-terrorist operation in Britain began.[24]

The second intervention came from Emma Wallis, of Access Self Storage, in west London. She alerted MI5 when three Muslim men placed a huge bag of fertiliser in a locker they had rented.[25] Police began a surveillance operation. They took the precaution of removing the fertiliser and replacing it with a harmless substance.

Disclosure of another serious intelligence failure came with the trial of four men who tried to carry out a suicide bomb attack in London on 21 July 2005. They were all convicted of conspiring to murder and cause explosions. Sentencing them at Woolwich Crown Court to life imprisonment on 11 July 2007, Mr Justice Fulford said they were controlled and directed by al-Qaeda. He ordered a re-trial in the cases of two co-defendants, Adel Yahya and Manfo Asiedu, about whom the jury was unable to reach a decision.[26] They denied conspiracy to murder.[27]

Later, the two were also jailed. Adel Yahya was sentenced to six years and nine months at the High Court in London on 5 November 2007, after pleading guilty to possessing terrorist information. He no longer faced a retrial for conspiracy to murder after the charge was dropped by the prosecution.[28] Manfo Asiedu was jailed for 33 years on 20 November 2007, after pleading guilty earlier at the Old Bailey to conspiring to cause explosions.[29]

He was sentenced at Kingston Crown Court for his part in helping to plan the failed suicide attacks on London's transport network. Asiedu was meant to have exploded his rucksack device but 'lost his nerve at the last moment' and dumped it in woodland, the court heard.[30] Muktar Said Ibrahim, Ramzi Mohammed, Yassin Omar and Hussain Osman were all sentenced to life imprisonment when they were convicted in July 2007. They were jailed for at least 40 years. But their home-made devices failed to explode and no-one was killed. Only two weeks before, four British Islamists had killed 52 people in suicide bombings in London.

When Muktar Said Ibrahim, ringleader of the plot, went to Pakistan, he was driven to Heathrow by a man already under scrutiny, and their car was followed.[31] Ibrahim was questioned by the Special Branch at the airport, but he was allowed freely back into Britain three months later. On his return, he was regarded as of less concern than some others under surveillance. His recruitment of his team and purchase of hydrogen peroxide to make bombs were not noticed.

Ibrahim was photographed by police at a training camp in the Lake District in May 2004. Three fellow plotters were also there.[32] Ibrahim was photographed again in August 2004 at Finsbury Park mosque in North London.

On 21 July 2005 the gang plotted to attack the city's transport system. Mr Justice Fulford said that had they succeeded at least 50 people would have died and hundreds been injured.[33] Peter Clarke, head of Scotland Yard's counter terrorism command, said the four men convicted of the 21/7 attempts 'failed to set off their bombs – not through want of trying'.[34]

Behind the failure to pick up Ibrahim and his fellow plotters, there is a deeper question – whether the work of Special Branch had been compromised by the drive for dominance by MI5.

The Special Branch, the world's oldest specialist force against political violence, ceded its main role in fighting mainland terrorism to MI5 in the early 1990s. The skills of the branch had been honed since its formation in 1883. On 8 September 2005 its demise and merger with other anti-terrorist police were announced. At the same time the police were having to make do with less money than they felt necessary to combat terrorism. MI5 and MI6 were to get the most.

Recent failures by MI5 to identify some recruits to al-Qaeda have raised concerns that sleepers who are trying to get jobs in the Security Service and police may not have been picked up. Both organisations are confident of their vetting procedures, but in June 2006 the Intelligence and Security Committee, which monitors MI5, alerted it to the risks associated with its rapid expansion.

Links with al-Qaeda gave a new dimension to the terrorist threat in the UK. Its deputy leader, Ayman al-Zawahiri, warned on 10 July 2007 of more bombing operations against Britain. The network inspired by Osama Bin Laden is still a menace with which we have to contend, as we will see in the next chapter. On 13 July 2007 the US Senate voted to double the reward against him to $50 million (£24.5 million).

Note on appeals:

Page 159: Omar Khyam's application for leave to appeal against conviction was refused. Waheed Mahmood and Jawad Akbar sought leave to appeal against conviction and sentence. Both were refused. The applications of Salahuddin Amin and Anthony Garcia to appeal against conviction and sentence were also refused. But the life sentence of Amin (with a recommended minimum term of 17 years and six months) has been changed to a life sentence with a minimum recommendation of 16 years and nine months. He was detained in Pakistan for 10 months, which counts as time served). The original life sentence of Garcia with a minimum recommended term of 20 years has been reduced to a life sentence with a minimum recommended term of 17 years and six months. Amin's lawyers were considering whether to pursue his case to the European Court in Strasbourg. All five had been found guilty of conspiracy to cause explosions likely to endanger life.

Page 166: Muktar Said Ibrahim, Yassin Omar, Hussain Osman and Ramzi Mohammed lost a Court of Appeal bid to challenge their convictions. Their applications for leave to appeal were rejected. Applications brought by Mohammed and Osman against their sentences were also dismissed.

Page 166: Manfo Asiedu was seeking leave to appeal against sentence. He was refused.

12

Bin Laden – a Force in British Politics

Whether liberties in Britain will be further curtailed depends to a large extent on Osama Bin Laden and al-Qaeda. They have become a force in British politics. The threat they pose has produced drastic action by the State, as we have seen. To assess the threat and the reaction to it, the strength and potential of the terrorists need to be understood. The old adage 'know your enemy' is never more important than in twenty-first-century Britain.

Peter Clarke, who led Scotland Yard's fight against the bombers, thought it was 'hopelessly optimistic' to expect that the threat from al-Qaeda could be contained within five or even ten years. Al-Qaeda is 'believed to have talked of plans over the next 50 years'. Clarke was speaking at the Royal United Services Institute on 16 February 2006.

Britain and the rest of the world will, therefore, remain for the indefinite future al-Qaeda's intended targets. Increasingly, the war in Iraq has been blamed for encouraging terrorism – criticism an angry President Bush has rejected. The conflict and the slaughter of civilians destabilised the region and the world. The policies of Blair and Bush were in disarray.

A damning blow to them came in a United States intelligence report[1] saying that the war in Iraq had become a 'cause célèbre for jihadists'. Extracts declassified by President Bush and released on 26 September 2006 said the conflict had bred a deep resentment of US involvement in the Muslim world. 'If this trend continues,

169

threats to US interests at home and abroad will become more diverse, leading to increasing attacks world-wide.'

The report was a consensus of 16 intelligence agencies, which also predicted further attacks in Europe as extremist networks inside the extensive Muslim diasporas there 'facilitate recruitment and staging'.

The US fight against al-Qaeda had enjoyed some successes, but these were outweighed by anti-Americanism, decentralised terrorist groups which were harder to penetrate and corruption in Muslim regimes, all of which encouraged the spread of al-Qaeda.

In Britain the number of young Muslims becoming radicalised worried the British Government and law enforcement agencies. Peter Clarke said on 3 September 2006 that thousands of British Muslims suspected of possible terrorist involvement were being watched by police and MI5. He was being interviewed for a BBC2 documentary 'al-Qaeda: Time to Talk'.

Muslims say that the alienated young want revenge for deaths from bombing in the Lebanon, from the invasion of Iraq and its aftermath and from persecution in Palestine. A survey of 1,000 young Muslims for a Channel Four Dispatches programme on 6 August 2006 showed that almost a quarter said the suicide bomb attacks of 7 July 2005 on London could be justified. A third would prefer to live under the strict Sharia law. Stonings are among its punishments. A third also had a wish to see Britain eventually become an Islamic State.

The gathering momentum has enabled terrorists in Britain to be better organised. Following the example of the Provisional IRA, cells were being led by a planner and a quartermaster for explosives, weapons and training. In other ways they were a bit like some of the tougher military units, with bonding and exposure to harsh conditions. Indoctrination is what makes Muslin recruits different. Fraud is used for funding. The development alarmed intelligence insiders into believing that Britain would continue to be a major target.

The most dangerous terrorists may lead outwardly normal lives until they kill without warning. Good intelligence is vital. The global threat has provided an excuse for a further tightening of laws which make inroads into civil liberties. Increased numbers of armed police officers are on watch in Britain. Security chiefs have been given scope which is unprecedented in modern times. The danger of terrorist attack against nuclear power stations is already a consideration in the debate about Britain's future energy policy. A Home Office Minister, Hazel Blears, told of contingency plans against chemical, biological, radiological or nuclear weapons. Measures were in place to counter electronic threats to vital networks which could disrupt industry, government and day-to-day living. The bigger the threat, the more that freedoms will be challenged.

This is the orthodoxy used, as by the Inquisition in the past, to reinforce fears of the unknown and stamp on deviancy. Torture produced confessions then, as it may now. Suspects were spied upon and whole communities were in danger of being tainted, as they may now be.

Sceptics today do not believe that the threat of terrorism is anything like as great as the authorities make out. Just as there was a vested interest in talking up the cold war threat as a means of investment in the arms race, so now MI5 and the rest of the security world are benefiting from the growth in surveillance, counter-intelligence and anti-terrorism measures across pretty well every activity in daily life. This is the heresy being expounded.

One heretic with his own views is Richard Jackson, a senior lecturer in international politics at Manchester University. He says that on a statistical scale, terrorism ranks somewhere around the risk of being killed in a home repairs accident or being struck by lightning. An article of his was being published in a book called *Playing Politics With Terrorism: A User's Guide*, edited by George Kassimeris.[2] Jackson told me: 'My feeling is that the expansion of State security will in the end be used for illiberal purposes and result in major human rights abuses, mainly because they will have to justify their own existence.'

Attempts to discover why Muslims in Britain have become

radicalised have concentrated on the younger generation today and not on their parents. The Pakistanis were always quick off the mark. Before barriers were put up against Commonwealth immigration in 1962 they were the swiftest to try and beat them. There were not even the beginnings of integration when I stayed in a Pakistani lodging house in Bradford in 1964 and learnt Muslim table manners, eating with a chapati shaped like a funnel to scoop up food, and using the correct hand for hygiene reasons. Workers in the woollen mills had been fetched via the family and village networks. These networks provided ethnic support and continued native customs. Little English was spoken and they were in the hands of their better equipped compatriots.

It is not surprising that young Muslims go to Pakistan, where they may have been indoctrinated. The links have always been strong. One Bradford Pakistani offered to take me there by van in 1965, smuggling tea on the way. *The Times* refused me permission. Many Pakistanis were despatched here by families to send money home. There was often not enough land to support a new generation of sons and, on a visit to the sub-continent I discovered how even the provision of a new water pump could make a vital difference. One elderly man proudly showed me his gas ring – a technological revolution paid for by his son in England. A pipe led to it from a tank of fermenting water buffalo manure behind his house. Since Indian money from England provided splendid temples, it would not surprise me if funds were provided for Mosques in Pakistan.

I discovered that Pakistanis were at that time the least inclined to fight for their rights when I initiated a Marplan survey of young immigrants for *The Times* in 1971. Ninety-one per cent of West Indians interviewed agreed strongly that 'he should be prepared to fight for his rights as a black man'. Comparable figures of strong feeling among Indians were 78 per cent and Pakistanis 50 per cent.[3]

The report, afterwards published in full by the Runnymede Trust, provided a prescient warning. The Pakistanis were the most depressed of the groups by British standards. They were the most culturally introverted and therefore some cause for concern. They were the least ambitious to better themselves.

> The Pakistanis are, therefore, the least inclined to a radical response. This does not mean their passivity can be relied upon to persist: a minority of the young are already becoming tinged by the host culture. Harassment and restriction of opportunity, even within their limited enclave, might be expected to suggest, ultimately a more active response.

That change has now come about dramatically.

There was some early controversy over Sikhs' turbans. They overcame any opposition in workplaces and elsewhere to wearing them. Otherwise Indians have not shown the same aggression as present day young Muslims. But Britain has not invaded the Punjab recently, and in India Israel is not much of a problem. The Indians also had a good start. The survey showed that, while 61 per cent of the Indians claimed to have one or more 'O' levels, this was true of only 9 per cent of Pakistanis.

Violence was submerged. As long ago as 1964 I was hijacked by two fanatical young Indians who leapt into the back of my car and said, in best Hollywood style: 'Drive on.' They wanted to know why I was examining their community. I explained I was writing about it to help create understanding and opportunities for people like them. After a quarter of an hour or so of touring around the town they leapt out at traffic lights as suddenly as they had arrived. A day or two later I found a razor sharp knife with a pale blue wooden handle under my driving seat.

For any ethnic group which feels itself socially and economically worse off than it should be, a strong leader prepared to put things right and preach the beliefs that will stir followers is welcomed. That is how most charismatic, populist leaders carry the masses with them. Even if Osama Bin Laden dies, his planned terrorist strategy will continue for as long as young al-Qaeda fanatics wish to pursue it. Religious wars are not new – only the intensity of the global threat today. The Thirty Years War in Europe in the seventeenth century, also over religion, involved Roman Catholics and Protestants. Pessimists believe that Bin Laden's holy war, which began ten years ago, is likely to last much longer. He wants to fulfil long-term strategic aims, hopelessly ambitious as they may be.

Bin Laden has become a world figure – an elusive wraith, creating worrying uncertainty. Analysts in MI5 and MI6 scan his reported words like textual scholars in search of authenticity and for clues to his intentions. Goebbels, Hitler's propaganda chief, would have been proud of his capacity to alarm his target audiences, yet claim justification for unspeakable acts. Today few people know as much about al-Qaeda as they did about the Nazis in the Second World War.

Words attributed to Bin Laden gather a force of their own. *Al-Jazeera*, the Arab news network, is one source which the media report internationally and the security services study. A revealing transcript of a speech (30 October 2004) says Bin Laden saw towers in Lebanon demolished in an Israeli attack helped by the American Sixth Fleet. 'It entered my mind that we should punish the oppressor in kind and that we should destroy towers in America in order that they taste some of what we tasted and so that they be deterred from killing our women and children.'[4]

Items like this, about Bin Laden and the twin towers, cannot be authenticated and differ widely, causing endless speculation. New York's twin towers were destroyed on September 11, 2001 and more than 2,900 people killed in symbolic revenge by hijacked aircraft.

There are constant attempts to hunt down Bin Laden and, if necessary, to kill him. Reports of his death from time to time raise hopes in the Pentagon and MI5 headquarters, but none has yet been substantiated. On 18 January 2006, *al-Jazeera* received a tape which the CIA thought to be of Bin Laden. It said that an attack on the United States had been prepared but proposed a truce to enable Iraq and Afghanistan to be rebuilt. He has vowed never to be taken alive. If he is killed, his perceived martyrdom will incite his vengeful followers.[5]

The report of the 9/11 Commission on terrorist attacks on the United States describes America's gradual awareness of the threat posed by Bin Laden. President Clinton's security advisor woke him at 5.35 a.m. on 7 August 1998 to tell him of the almost simultaneous bombings of the US embassies in Nairobi, Kenya, and Dar-es-Salaam, Tanzania. 'Suspicions quickly focused on Bin Laden. Unusually good intelligence, chiefly from the year-long monitoring of al-Qaeda's cell in Nairobi, soon firmly fixed responsibility on him and his associates.'[6]

He has since exasperated President George W. Bush, who would dearly love 'to smoke him out'. Bin Laden has good intelligence and political timing. He noted on his 18 January tape that a British memorandum had been leaked with the allegation that Bush had suggested to Tony Blair bombing *al-Jazeera*'s offices, the source of information amplified by media throughout the world. Misjudgements like this are seized upon and bring recruits flocking to al-Qaeda's cause.

No action, however, has been of more help to the terrorists than the Iraq war. A warning by analysts on MI5's official website after the London bombings concluded: 'Though they have a range of aspirations and 'causes', Iraq is a dominant issue for a range of extremist groups and individuals in the UK and Europe.'[7]

This is not what some politicians would wish to hear. Operations in Iraq were supposed to be part of the war against terror. MI5 added: 'Some individuals who support the insurgency are known to have travelled to Iraq in order to fight against coalition forces. In the longer term, it is possible that they may later return to the UK and consider mounting attacks here.'

Even more chilling was a video of Mohammad Sidique Khan, the British-born ringleader of the bombing attack on London, blaming his country's foreign policy. The explosions on a bus and three underground trains were the result of the British government continuing to commit 'atrocities' against Muslims, Khan said, with evident

175

reference to Iraq and Palestine. The tapes, which were aired by *al-Jazeera* and reported in an official British account of the bombings, implied that al-Qaeda claimed responsibility for the attacks, something which intelligence analysts had not previously acknowledged. As if to reinforce the impression, a second video, of al-Qaeda's second in command, Ayman al-Zawahiri, was shown.[8] Thirty-year-old Khan, a former classroom assistant, died with six victims on a train at Edgware Road tube station when he triggered a bomb.

British Intelligence chiefs had warned before the attacks that the risk of terrorism in Britain was increased by the war in Iraq, according to a leak to the *New York Times*.[9] But they found that no group currently had the 'intent and the capability' to mount an attack. The intelligence report was written only three weeks before the attacks.

The battle for Iraq was regarded as crucial to the war against terror. But, far from quelling it, there was, as we have seen, firm evidence that George W. Bush has put the world further at risk.

Tony Blair must have been aware of high level concern in Whitehall that the Iraq war was fuelling Muslim extremism in Britain, because the Foreign Office's top official, Sir Andrew Turnbull, told 10 Downing Street so in a letter before the London bombings. The letter was reported in the *Observer* of 28 August 2005.[10] Attached to it was a strategy document which said Britain was now viewed as a 'crusader state', on a par with America as a potential target.

Reinforcing memories which have significance for the Muslim mind and spirit, George Bush clumsily sabotaged his own 'war against terror'. Five days after the 9/11 attacks he promised retaliation, and referred to a 'crusade' which, although a figure of speech, had bloody historic resonance.

Tony Blair, also a religious man, annoyed Muslims by invoking God on ITV on 4 March 2006 as his judge for the attack on Iraq. He explained how he could live with going to war. 'If you have faith about these things then you realise that judgement is made by other people. If you believe in God, it's made by God as well.'[11]

Mr Blair has called up a belief in God in a way which to Islamist fundamentalists is provocative. He is 'a polytheist' in the words of Zengi, a famous twelfth-century Muslim warrior. And 'polytheists' fought in the Crusades, just as Islamic extremists will say 'polytheists' are fighting now in Iraq and Afghanistan.

The word was synonymous with 'Crusaders', which was how Bin Laden saw Britain and the United States. The term provided historic justification for Islamist terrorists. It ascribed to the West bloody aspirations which hark back to the Middle Ages when knights from all over Europe fought with ruthless fervour to safeguard the Holy Land for Christendom.

Most people think of the 'gentil parfait knights' of Chaucer playing against Muslims with the chivalry later attributed to them. By contrast, today's militant Muslims have a longer memory which cannot be understood without reference to at least the siege of Jerusalem in July 1099. When the victorious Crusaders had fought their way into the citadel, they indulged in an orgy of murder, slaughtering both Muslims and Jews. Estimates of the men, women and children killed vary from 'hundreds' to most of the 70,000 population.

Raymond of Aguilers saw 'God's vengeance' at work:

It is sufficient to relate that, in the Temple of Solomon (the Aqsa mosque) and the portico, the crusaders rode in blood to the knees and bridles of their horses. In my opinion this was poetic justice that the Temple of Solomon should receive the blood of pagans who blasphemed God there for many years. Jerusalem was now littered with bodies and stained with blood... A new day, new gladness, new and everlasting happiness, and the fulfilment of our toil and love brought forth new words and songs for all.'[12]

The Islamic counter-attacks during the crusades were led by warriors fighting a war even more fanatically religious than now. Today, forces from the West are again seen to be threatening Muslim interests. The notorious Osama Ben Laden of his day was Zengi, mentioned in *Crusades*. Bin Laden's utterances, meeting a different challenge, are to do with a global struggle. A *madrasa* (religious college) at Damascus bears an inscription of 1138, describing Zengi as 'the fighter of *jihad*, the defender of the frontier, the tamer of the polytheists (Christians) and destroyer of the heretics'. One Muslim chronicler said: 'He was tyrannical and he would strike with indiscriminate recklessness. He was like a leopard ... like a lion in fury, not renouncing any severity, not knowing any kindness.' There were atrocities on both sides.

Bin Laden's early hatred of the United States developed into terrorism at the time of the Gulf war, although it was too early then for MI5 to anticipate the implications for Britain. When Saddam Hussein invaded Kuwait in 1990, Bin Laden's request to the Saudi Government to allow him to mobilise *jihadists* against the Iraqis was refused. He was outraged when a US coalition force, including other non-Muslims, was based in Saudi Arabia, home of some of Islam's holiest places. They brought with them a life-style from an infidel culture he despised.

He was already experienced in recruiting and organising fighters against an outside enemy. Money from the family business, one of the largest in Saudi Arabia, provided the means to back Muslim guerrillas, the *mujahideen*, against the Soviet invaders of Afghanistan in 1979. To do so, Bin Laden founded a group called Maktab al-Khadamat. Recruits came from around the world. Various sources are quoted on whether or not the group was given US support, perhaps indirectly, but the official American line is strongly to deny that it aided future terrorists.

Bin Laden displayed the skills of a diplomat – 'the art of letting the other fellow have your own way' – between fractious Afghan fighters, and struck up a wary understanding with Mullah Mohamed Omar, the Taliban's most influential head. An early spiritual guide had been Abdullah Azzam, Hamas's founder, whose preaching fired Bin Laden's religious enthusiasm when he was still a student. In Pakistan where they met, he learnt to lead fighters. Skill with a gun came naturally to him, and he is said to have won admiration for his determined coolness under Soviet fire.

With the Gulf war over, Bin Laden condemned the Saudi monarchy for allowing non-Muslim bases on its soil. This fired the anger of Islamist militants associated with him. Many of them had fought in the Afghan war and now came under his wing in Saudi Arabia. They were to fight in other places of conflict, including Bosnia. Thus al-Qaeda began to form. Bin Laden's expulsion by the Government to Sudan in 1991, far from quelling his ambitions, allowed him to use family money to back Sudanese aspirations and fund training camps, staffed by his old allies the *mujahideen*. As has since become apparent among activists everywhere, including bombers in Britain, Islamic studies forged a fervent sense of purpose and identity. Drawn to it, recruits came from many countries. Al-Qaeda's headquarters were established in Khartoum.

Egypt, target of successive terrorist attacks, was one source of recruitment for al-Qaeda. As in armies everywhere, training camps taught fighting skills and Bin Laden used money to promote an Islamic state. He can plausibly and deviously pretend to be as his audience would wish, while remaining a cold-blooded killer without remorse. He can switch, chameleon-like, from warlike aggression to peaceful benevolence, mixing courteously with all classes although intellectually superior to most. A ruthless murderer to the West, he was an inspirational leader to militant Muslims on the eve of action. Bin Laden was blamed for attacks on Saudi Arabia and US military bases in Dahran and Riyadh. The Saudi Government removed his citizenship.

Bin Laden became too hot to handle in the Sudan and was expelled in 1996 to Afghanistan where, aided by the credibility he had gained against the Soviets, he linked with the Taliban and provided money and battle-hardened men. As in the Sudan, he believed in training, which later benefited British Muslims coming to Pakistan to learn their skills. The defeat of the Taliban by the US drove him out, but his growing reputation attracted to him leaders of al-Jihad, exiled from Egypt, and he began to see his struggle as on an international scale. But MI5 did not at that stage foresee the full implications of its potential for Britain.

From now on Bin Laden's murderous tentacles would spread. An early attack on innocent civilians, which Bin Laden is suspected of funding, killed 67 tourists in Luxor, Egypt in 1997. President Bill Clinton froze his assets and authorised his arrest or assassination. Cruise missiles were launched by the US against him in 1998 but killed 19 others.

His ambitious goal is to see Israel destroyed and Americans ejected from Muslim countries, ending what he sees as their danger to Islamic identity and values. He also wants to remove pro-US leaders and with them America's political influence.

The date of 1982, when he saw the towers destroyed in Lebanon, also marks his parting from his family background. His father was involved in construction, and Bin Laden's degree from King Abdulaziz University, Jeddah, the previous year, followed study in, appropriately, business and project administration. But the projects became terror and the business was funding it. His father, who died in 1967, left him shares in the family company.

His lonely path has estranged him from not only his country but also his family. Said to have been born in 1957, he was at his son's wedding in 2001, but is reported to have met his mother only once since the attack on the two towers in New York. Among the rhetoric seeping from the Middle East, is a claim that his group had chemical and biological weapons which it intended to use against the United States and Israel.

Bin Laden does not have detailed control over al-Qaeda's operations. It is not based on territory, which distinguishes it from Basque, Irish or Algerian terrorists. Support for training and finance and other needs comes from higher up, particularly for big operations like those against New York's twin towers. As in wartime resistance against the Germans, it is not considered wise to know too much about those involved in other cells. This makes them harder for MI5 and police to eradicate. Whether or not a terrorist act is carried out by a known al-Qaeda cell does not matter too much to those

13

The Doomsday Scenario

The most disturbing reason for the restrictions on freedoms in Britain was given by John Reid, when Defence Secretary. He spoke of an enemy unashamedly determined to obtain chemical, biological or radiological weaponry to kill millions. To deal with the threat, he said, laws had been changed – for example the maximum period of detention before charge. The balance between freedom and security needed to be continually reviewed.

His words were more apocalyptic even than Enoch Powell's notorious 'rivers of blood speech', when he seemed to see the River Tiber foaming with much blood, as an outcome of racial strife. Powell fought in the 1939 war for freedoms under threat, and would no doubt have been fighting for them now – I knew him professionally and reported his words.

John Reid's address at the Royal United Services Institute for Defence Studies on 3 April 2006, was made against a background of increased State power, rising discontent about curbs on liberties and preparations to deal with chemical, biological, radiological or nuclear (CBRN) attack.

The Home Office said there were:

- 360 mobile decontamination units around the country for ambulance and accident and emergency departments.
- 7,250 personal protection suits for key health workers, with another 2,500 ones stockpiled by the State.

- Stockpiles of emergency medical equipment, strategically stored around the country and available at 24 hours' notice.
- 7,000 police officers specially trained to deal with CBRN incidents.
- 4,400 new high-performance anti-gas suits for fire fighters.[1]

Emergency action, guided by scientific and technological research, would include arranging urgent medical aid for casualties. Victims and the affected area would be decontaminated. The police and fire service had training, support and equipment centres, backed by an emergency planning college.

The question is whether the fear of attack justifies the threat to rights, some of which go back to the Middle Ages. Weapons grade nuclear material is seldom smuggled, according to experts, although other items are more of a menace, including medical waste. The so-called 'dirty bomb' is not all that it seems. Explosives in it would be more lethal than, say, the spent nuclear fuel with which they can be combined. Radio-activity could, however, cause the fear required by terrorists.

From time to time there are stories of terrorists trying to get hold of the right nuclear ingredients or smuggle them into the United States, or get tuition from experts in assembling a bomb. The International Atomic Energy Agency reported more than 400 occasions in four years on which smugglers were picked up. Would-be terrorists do regard radio-activity as a possibility.

The need for all emergency service personnel to be equipped to deal with radio-active substances was borne out by the mysterious case of the Russian, Alexander Litvinenko, in London. He died from the effects of polonium-210. Two detectives investigating his death were reported to have been contaminated.

However, polonium-210, like a dirty bomb, is not thought to be a favoured weapon of mass destruction or even preferred as a less destructive kind. Since weapons-grade nuclear material is rarely smuggled, the nuclear threat to the populace begins to sound less than it seemed, and mainly psychological. The case for sacrificing our liberties on that score is therefore diminished.

What else supported Mr Reid's argument for changes in the law to save the nation? Still on the agenda are biological weapons, the cyber war, radiology and defence against a chemical attack. It turned out that the police raid in Forest Gate, east London, prompted by a mistaken tip-off about the presence of chemicals, was not worth the infringement of liberty it caused. All the raid did was annoy many Muslims and, although the impetus for it came from MI5, the judgement of the police was criticised.

Biological weapons are the worst. They include bacteria or a virus and toxins and poisons with a biological derivation. They range from anthrax and Black Death, horrific in the fourteenth century, to smallpox and yellow fever, with a familiar range of diseases that were around in my childhood, like diphtheria and other potential killers.

Because chemical weapons disperse they do not persist like biological agents which can spread death in the right conditions. Sarin, the feared nerve agent, is calculated to be much less potent than botulinum toxin. It asphyxiates, taking its time.

Intelligence agencies look out for unusual attempts to hire crop-spraying aircraft or drones, which terrorists could use to deposit death over towns. They could also do so from the ground. To work, the spray would have to be reduced to a fine mist. Rain and high wind would best be avoided. A concentrated attack with a killer substance is one fear. Hospitals would be hard pressed to cope if the killer worked. Unless medicines were stockpiled across the country for a whole range of potential weapons – which is hardly possible – treatment would be limited in the event of an organised and determined assault.

Smallpox could be a suicide weapon. Suicide terrorists know that infecting themselve with smallpox and travelling on long distance aeroplanes to allow the air-conditioning to spread the disease would kill innumerable people. Another version in their potential armoury would be an attack with specially made aerosols to spread the virus by air or by touch.

Attacking strategic food or water supplies with biological weapons poses problems for mass contamination. It it is not easily done. Dead animals were used in the ancient world to infect wells. Infecting farm animals with BSE or foot and mouth disease would disrupt food supplies.

In an official war game exercise called 'Dark Winter' in 2001, a simulated release of smallpox in three US shopping malls, one of them in Oklahoma City, resulted in its being spread notionally in only 13 days to 25 states and 15 countries. The estimates are that a third of the many thousands who were 'infected' would have died. Panic-stricken refugees from the disease would find borders closed. National Guardsmen were theoretically allowed to use weapons on the border between Texas and Oklahoma.

The highly reputable ANSER Institute for Homeland Security, which was one of the sponsors for the exercise, concluded that a major biological attack could cause massive civilian casualties, a breakdown in essential institutions and civil disorder. Americans were unprepared for it. The Government was not equipped to handle such a catastrophe. US healthcare would be overwhelmed by a widespread epidemic.[2]

In the cyber war the defences are technical, relying on management alertness and expertise to prevent terrorists sabotaging the systems on which advanced countries now rely. An appropriate equivalent is needed of Professor R.V. Jones's brilliant scientific counter-measures in the 1939 war which put enemy raiders off course and camouflaged allied intentions. The war against Germany was largely a nationalised industry, but the electronic war against terrorism is today mostly private enterprise.

Stocks of more than 100 types of deadly viruses and bacteria in Britain have been given added security. Staff and laboratories would be officially vetted in pharmaceutical companies, hospitals and universities which handled the agents.

Surveillance suggested that suspected al-Qaeda associates were training to attack vital electronic networks in economic, medical and transport targets. There is no end to the choice for sabotage. One intriguing suggestion was that dams, once the target of the

RAF's dam-busters' squadron, might have systems which could be taken over electronically to open floodgates. The defence of the nuclear industry is vital. Only a terrorist would want a repeat of the Chernobyl disaster. The combination of a bomb and electronic attack on the emergency services' control systems would be disastrous.

The cyber-war against terrorists could, at worst, be more destructive of our way of life than bombing, although not as bloody. These days, one signalling failure on the railway can cause localised chaos, but imagine what it would be like if a whole system were knocked out. Add to that air traffic control, hospitals, power stations, banking and the rest of the organisations we rely on. The worst case scenario is that we would be returned to the eighteenth century in a trice, without the means to cope with it.

Our society has become a hostage to the computer and to those who install systems and sometimes get them wrong. It occurred to me that electronic warfare might have been used to destroy Iraq's infrastructure and enable Britain and America to take over without so much bloodshed. An absence of death and destruction would have deprived the suicide bombers of some of their motivation and saved thousands of lives.

However, that was not possible. Iraq is not as vulnerable to electronic attack as more advanced countries. Terrorists have had to make do with mass murder intended to provoke a civil war, which would threaten its neighbours and pro-Western oil suppliers. Computerisation is not a priority of the Iraqi government or its main political parties. Sanctions, rather than the Iraq–Iran war, held back computerisation within Iraq government departments and within daily life itself.

An example of potential damage was the attack on HM Coastguard in 2004 by the Sasser worm virus. A press notice from the Maritime and Coastguard Agency on 4 May 2004 gave valuable insight into emergency procedures, as a result of which services were largely unaffected.

Her Majesty's Coastguard continually practise for events such as these and when databases and other computer held information began to go off-line this morning a paper-based system known colloquially as 'pinkies' began to be put into effect.

This system was in use before the more widespread use of computers and has served the Coastguard well over many years. Currently computer aided maps have been set aside in favour of manual map reading and the Coastguard will need to contact other services for accurate database retrieval whilst its own systems are down.[3]

Peter Dymond, head of search and rescue at the agency, stated:

Radio and other forms of communication from ships at sea remain unaffected and despite the problems that this bug has given us this morning and the way it might hinder our access of information, we remain confident that by telephone and other means of communication we can ensure that no rescue or incident will be affected. Our IT department are working hard to bring the rest of the agency – and coastguard stations – back online during the rest of the day.[4]

Three years later Estonia accused Russia of attacking central websites and its infrastructure, but firm proof of the perpetrators' identity was never produced. The assault followed a government decision to remove a war memorial to the Red Army from Tallinn, the capital. Targets for the cyber raiders included banks, newspapers, government ministries and public services. If Russia had been really to blame, it would have been the first such attack by one country against another, but whether a computer assault by a belligerent State would count as an act of war is something for international lawyers to consider.

Britain is not immune. Computer systems of top legal firms, banks and accountants reportedly faced possible espionage attack from Chinese state organisations. Rolls-Royce and Shell were said to have been targeted.

The Computer Crime Research Center quoted US officials as

saying that data from computers seized in Afghanistan indicated that al-Qaeda had reconnoitered systems that control American energy facilities, water distribution, communication systems and other parts of the infrastructure.

For the terrorist there are striking advantages in using electronic attacks. In an article for the Center, Mudawi Mukhtar Elmusharaf says they are cheaper, tracking them is difficult, names and places can be hidden, there are no physical barriers or check points to cross, attacks can be made remotely from anywhere in the world, many targets can be attacked and people affected. Targets could include natural gas flows, financial institutions, telephones and air traffic control and energy systems.[6]

The Government's strategy is to defend what is called 'the critical national infrastructure' (CNI), which sustains the life of the nation. Any entire or partial loss or compromise could:

- cause large-scale loss of life;
- have a serious impact on the national economy;
- have other grave social consequences for the community;
- be of immediate concern to national government.

The critical national infrastructure consists of ten interdependent sectors: communications, emergency services, energy, finance, food, government and public service, health, public safety, transport and water. The details were provided by the National Infrastructure Co-ordinating Centre (NISCC), now merged into a joint body.

Each sector comprised many different companies and organisations, all of which relied heavily on computers and associated technologies in their day-to-day business, making them vulnerable to electronic attack. A direct route to them was provided by the internet, which was used to aid business efficiency.

Unauthorised access to the data or control software of systems would allow intruders to acquire or corrupt the data or disrupt its functioning. Their aim would be 'denial of service' (DOS), usually by hacking or the insertion of malicious software or hardware.

189

Hacking means any attempt to gain unpermitted access to a computer system. Malicious viruses, worms and trojans use e-mails to gain entry. Illicit hardware modifications are normally carried out before installation or during maintenance. Attacks to deny use overwhelm systems with a flood of unwanted information. Waves of attacks can be mounted. The tools to do so are widely available and obtainable on the internet. Sophisticated attacks are unlikely to be detected by routine defences.

The size of the task to protect computers from malicious intrusion is shown by the Centre:

> Any system connected directly or indirectly to the internet or public networks is at risk. Indeed, insecurity is virtually built into most computer systems. Being designed primarily to store, retrieve and share information, mechanisms for protection and denial tend to be less fundamental to the system.[7]

The threat, as stated by official agencies, makes the measures outlined by Government to pick up terrorists involved hardly foolproof. They can attack from anywhere in the world. They are not carrying any obvious equipment. Stopping and searching willy-nilly will not find any tools for the job, if the terrorist is going to attack secretly from a hidden computer elsewhere. Only if detected, which is difficult, would the pressure be on him from tougher measures. The real defences are technical and managerial.

The need for constant vigilance is shown by an alleged plot to attack a crucial nerve centre for the internet in Britain which would have disrupted business in the City of London and elsewhere. David Leppard wrote in *The Sunday Times* on 11 March 2007 that detectives had found evidence of the alleged plot in a series of raids. Telehouse Europe, in Docklands, said it was on 'a heightened state of alert'. It provides back-up in case of terrorist attack elsewhere.

As with all crime prevention, good intelligence is the key to anticipating biological or chemical attack. A warning for world intelligence agencies was sounded in 1995 with an attack using

14

Defusing the Time-bomb

Moves for stronger oversight of MI5, long overdue, were made by Gordon Brown as one of his first initiatives as Prime Minister.

The Intelligence and Security Committee was discredited by its previous failure to call MI5 properly to account over the London bombings. It reported to Tony Blair. The government was consulting on how in future the Committee should be appointed and report to Parliament. Where possible, hearings should be in public. Mr Brown wished there to be better investigations, reports to be subject to longer Parliamentary debate and greater transparency over appointments to the committee. Another idea, that heads of MI5 and MI6 should be available for questioning in public by MPs and Peers, has been considered. The question was whether the government really had the will to bring about reforms.

A momentum was building for the use of intercept evidence in court, although it would be against the wishes of those opponents in MI5 and its friends who do not see why anyone else should hear their secrets, even if justice suffers by their reticence.

This book has produced evidence to show how ineffectual the previous oversight of MI5 was. One of its worst effects was the refusal by most Muslims to believe what MI5 said. Yet it was in the hearts and minds of such people that Mr Brown wished to increase confidence in the British system.

According to a survey of 500 British Muslims, commissioned by Channel 4 News with GFK NOP, 52 per cent believed that the

British security services had made up evidence to convict terrorist suspects. Fifty-nine per cent believed that the government had not told the public the whole truth about the 7 July bombings. Twenty-four per cent believed that the men identified as the 7 July bombers were not actually responsible for the attacks. A quarter believed that the authorities were involved in staging the London bombings.[1]

The findings of the poll reveal a massive distrust in MI5 and the authorities which Mr Brown's measures would have to tackle if dangerous alienation was not to worsen. One Muslim interviewed on Channel 4 News reminded viewers of the miscarriages of justice over the Guildford Four and Birmingham Six. Since MI5 takes the lead in terrorist intelligence it cannot escape some responsibility. If MI5 is to win trust in the Muslim community, much greater accountability is essential.

One way in which doubts over suspects could be dispelled would be to give them a proper trial. The absence of intercept evidence has interfered with the court systems. Justice was not seen to be done, and fed Muslim resentments. The ban on intercept evidence was encouraged by MI5's worried lobbying. It had as much to do with protecting MI5's operational methods from scrutiny as any outside threat to security,

In their drive to bring terrorists to justice the police had wanted to use intercept evidence that was otherwise hidden in MI5 files. Such evidence is available in terrorist and organised crime cases in the USA. Among those in Britain said to want the ban lifted were Lord Goldsmith, the Attorney General; Sir Ian Blair, Metropolitan Police Commissioner; and Sir Ken Macdonald, Director of Public Prosecutions. But GCHQ didn't like the idea, believing time and money would have to be spent on transcripts.

Pressure has been growing for stricter accountability by MI5. Intelligence-led forays into the Muslim community, based on flawed information, can be a cause of deep resentment and hinder the longer-term need to bring Muslims into the wider community.

MI5 has not the same experience as the police force, and lacks its discipline. It should be less wayward and as accountable as the police are, and should come under the scrutiny of the Chief Inspector of Constabulary. He or she should issue an annual report on MI5 and be able to order independent investigations into it. The present ineffective Intelligence and Security Committee is not knowledgeable enough about operational techniques. An Inspector of Constabulary, one of the Chief Inspector's deputies, should maintain day-to-day observation of MI5 and make recommendations. All information should go to a Minister who should be responsible to Parliament. Lines of responsibility for and by MI5 have been tangled and confusing.

The government's bureaucratic initiatives, which seek to influence the police but in reality get in their way, should be kept in reserve. Lord Denning's fine principles should be reasserted. The chief constable should be answerable to the law, not to ministers or to the bureaucracy. He should enforce the law, and with it the freedom that comes under the law. We do not want a state police. They should be brought to book if they go outside the law.

MI5 should have no influence over chief constables. MI5's influence over decisions which result in suspects being held is questionable and should be monitored by the Chief Inspector of Constabulary and referred, if necessary, to the appropriate Chief Constable. Telephone interceptions should be used in court evidence, regardless of MI5's opinion, so that decisions about detaining suspected terrorists could be brought into the open and justice seen to be done. They deserve to be dealt with in a safe and proper way, not held by control orders that cannot be properly enforced without infringements of human rights.

MI5 does not like its work to be properly assessed, whether in general concerning its failures before the London bombings or over information gained by torture, or in particular over whether innocent people are being wrongly detained without proper trial. *Habeas corpus* is more important than MI5, and MI5 should be put in its place. Also, while we are about it, there is a place in modern society for the Anglo-Saxon law against eavesdropping, or, at least, against eavesdropping that is not properly controlled.

The police, the judges and the magistrates are in the end there to guarantee freedom. They should be encouraged to defend it, against terrorists and criminals, to safeguard the vulnerable and to protect the Queen's Peace, a noble aim. The defence of the realm, with which MI5 concerns itself, is the business of the State, not the people. The *Shorter Oxford English Dictionary* defines 'realm' as 'a kingdom... Also any region or territory, esp. of a specified ruling power; the sphere, domain or province of some quality, state, or other abstract conception'.[3] Perhaps to that long list of responsibilities MI5 might like to add four other words: 'The defence of liberty'?

The key to peace is joined-up intelligence and joined-up policy. Inbred MI5 ought to liaise better with MI6 in a more systematic and organised way under an effective joint controller. Their identities, terms of employment and budgets could be kept separate.

The real test for Gordon Brown was if he could give people the peace to live their lives in private. The many CCTV cameras and monitoring of road users are part of a pattern of surveillance which, with the use of mobile phones and bank cards, will tell those in authority where you have been and what you have been up to. CCTV cameras with loudspeakers enable a distant official to boom directions at individuals committing minor misdemeanours. A spy in the sky will now be available to police and MI5 – a robot drone deployed over streets, housing estates and open country with the aim (of course) of watching for crime and terrorism. There will be no escape from the surreptitious, persistent watching eye.

Solitariness, privacy, escape, reticence, confidentiality or a wish simply to be alone are qualities prized in a civilised society, but they are being destroyed by official intrusion into daily life. You are no longer a private individual.

Your computer will be a useful target for the prying State intent, of course, on preventing terrorism. This chapter of the book you are now reading suddenly disappeared from my computer systems without trace, although I had 'saved' it. A computer expert could not explain why, nor why my recent month's e-mails disappeared and were hidden elsewhere in the computer's memory among items to be deleted. We, of course, blame the machine, although an earlier chapter discloses more sinister occurrences. (Fortunately, I had saved the missing words on a CD.)

Institutions are under attack by the State. The Privy Council, which is being bureaucratised, is more than merely ceremonial. It is a body enjoying historical significance with a job to do, and is part of the roots and identity of the nation and of the monarchy, which is its symbolic pinnacle.

Decision-takers like General Sir Mike Jackson are being hindered by the bureaucratic State. They need enough freedom to lead, but this is being stifled. If Generals do not have charge of their budgets – his complaint – how can they be responsible for the well-being of their troops, their morale and the equipment that will save lives and win battles? The alternative kills soldiers.

The bureaucracy, like entwining tree roots, is interfering with doctors, judges, magistrates and chief constables – all valued people in the institutions which keep this country working sensibly. Major planning decisions, which have previously allowed a more persistent democratic right to object, were to be speeded up by being put in the hands of a new commission. The aim was to make decisions faster so that the economy could benefit – an aim which appeared to put people second. Bearing in mind previous planning controversies, direct action could result. Riots are the voice of the unheard, said Martin Luther King, in words which have general significance.

Meanwhile spying will get a boost in Home Office proposals for public bodies to tell police or 'other relevant authority' if they become concerned about an individual. The idea would be to assess risk and refer the case to a multi-agency body. The object is to prevent serious violence.

MI5 can be understood only as part of the bureaucracy, with its involvement in control orders and interminable report writing and data storage. It is part of the apparatus of the State. An equivalent in another country would be regarded as the secret police. Yet every country needs them, in some form, and has to come to terms with them, these days as a weapon against terrorists. The problem arises if they cannot come to terms with their country's social or political needs, and if they use their powers illegitimately for their own agenda. Bugging, shadowing people, phone tapping, use of informers and secret cameras keep intelligence analysts busy.

The surveillance society, of which MI5 is part, is supposedly a weapon against terrorism, but can be against deviant behaviour. The terrorist threat to the nation, told in blood-curdling terms, is often an alibi for over-reaction. It is true, however, that Britain's infrastructure is vulnerable. Attacks may come from anywhere in the world, which electronics have shrunk. Images from the Iraq war or Lebanon have caused instant outrage among young Muslims, have moved them to become terrorists and are used by terrorists to make chilling statements on television. Islamist Big Brothers, with their hostages on display, wish to frighten and intimidate.

The biggest question of all is how to defuse Islamist terror. British ministers are quietly dropping use of the pejorative term 'war on terror' – a favourite phrase of President Bush. The example of Northern Ireland has shown how patient negotiation and conciliation can, in certain circumstances, succeed in bringing peace, and with it a wary relaxation of security. Finding the right formula for 'peace' in the 'war against terror' might restore freedoms, loosen restrictions and help the nation to feel less edgy.

The first requirement is to do what might seem impossible for the non-Muslim, or even for the non-militant Muslim – to get into the mind of the suicide bomber to discover what motivates him when he detonates the explosive to commit mass murder.

The nearest to achieving that objective was a remarkable insight published in *The New Yorker* (19 November 2001).[4] A Muslim from Pakistan, Nasra Hassan interviewed nearly 250 people involved in the most militant Palestinian camps. They were failed suicide bombers, families of dead bombers and the men who trained them.

'Our meetings, which were arranged by intermediaries of all kinds, took place late at night, in back rooms, in small local cafés, on the sewage strewn Gaza beach, or in prison cells...'

One would-be suicide bomber had been pronounced brain dead from a bullet in the head, but nevertheless recovered. He was celebrated as a young man 'who gave his life to Allah' and whom Allah brought back to life.' Before his suicide mission he was in a constant state of worship. Asked what the attraction of martyrdom was, he said:

> The power of the spirit pulls us upward, while the power of material things pulls us downward. Someone bent on martyrdom becomes immune to the material pull ... We were floating, swimming, in the feeling that we were about to enter eternity. We had no doubts. We made an oath on the Koran, in the presence of Allah – a pledge not to waver. This jihad pledge is called *bayt al ridwan*, after the garden in Paradise that is reserved for the prophets and the martyrs. I know that there are other ways to do *jihad*. But this one is sweet – the sweetest. All martyrdom operations, if done for Allah's sake, hurt less than a gnat's bite.

An Imam affiliated to Hamas explained that the first drop of blood shed by a martyr during *jihad* washed away his sins instantaneously. 'On the Day of Judgement, he will face no reckoning. On the Day of Resurrection, he can intercede for seventy of his nearest and dearest to enter Heaven; and he will have at his disposal seventy-two houris, the beautiful virgins of Paradise.'

One volunteer said of the immediacy of Paradise: 'It is very, very near – right in front of our eyes. It lies beneath the thumb. On the other side of the detonator.'

Intense spiritual exercises were part of preparation for a mission. The candidate was encouraged to read in the Koran themes such as *jihad*, the birth of the nation of Islam, war, Allah's favours and the importance of faith. Religious lectures lasted from two to four hours each day. The living martyr went on lengthy fasts and spent much of the night praying. He paid off all his debts and asked for forgiveness for actual or perceived offences.

199

In the days before the mission, the candidate prepared a will on paper, audiocassette or video, sometimes all three, shot against a background of the sponsoring organisation's banner and slogans. To encourage him to confront death, not fear it, he repeatedly watched videos of himself and those of his predecessors.

Before his final journey, he performed a ritual ablution, put on clean clothes and tried to attend at least one communal prayer in the mosque. He said the traditional Islamic prayer that was customary before battle, and asked Allah to forgive his sins and bless his mission. He put a Koran in his left breast pocket, above the heart, and strapped the explosive round his waist or took with him a bag containing the bomb. The planner bade him farewell with the words: 'May Allah be with you, may Allah give you success, so that you achieve Paradise.' The would-be martyr responded: 'Inshallah, we will meet in Paradise.'

Hours later, as he pressed the detonator, he said: '*Allahu akbar* – Allah is great. All praise to him.'

Nasra Hassan's research was done in the Gaza strip. The enemy was Israel and hatred of it came from the provocations the people said they had suffered. Elsewhere, the essential spiritual motivation of the suicide bomber, for whatever earthly reason, may not be so ritualised, but in providing justification is as intense.

The intelligence agencies have made little public contribution to understanding terrorists or the causes of terrorism, only to its horrific effects. They are more concerned with the waves breaking on the shore than the great underlying currents.

Without understanding the sort of people likely to become terrorists, MI5 will not be able to stop them. Officers will not know where to look or see danger signals. Al-Qaeda can identify potential recruits, as terrorist threats to Britain repeatedly show. The only sound basis for analysing Muslim extremism is to compare it with other kinds and see what they have in common.

We know that Muslims hate alien secular domination, epitomised by the Coca-Cola culture and McDonald's American identity. Not only do they see them as a threat to their own way of life, but as

200

part of worldwide standardisation which swamps national identity and has been a growing cause of protest. Identity is about territory, language, race and religion. The key to understanding the conflicts they give rise to, involving not only Muslims, but people around the globe, can be summed up in a sentence. When identity is threatened people assert their identity in response to the threat. That is what Osama Bin Laden did. He and other fervent Muslims believed that Western, American-led culture was destroying their own. And they have bloodily asserted their own identity, seeking the ancient purity of Islam.

Conflict has been caused historically in Britain, though for similar reasons, less obviously. The investiture of the Prince of Wales produced direct action. Here was an expression of the identity of the United Kingdom, with a symbolism going back to the subjection of the Welsh by Edward I who built the castle where the investiture took place. A small minority of Welsh people, who resented Edward I and the subjugation of the land of their fathers, behaved true to form for the investiture. They asserted their identity in response to the ancient 'threat', and security forces were put on the alert against terrorism.

The royal train en route to Caernarfon was halted after a dummy bomb was found beneath a railway bridge. Two Royal Navy minesweepers patrolled the entrance to Caernarfon harbour. A team of frogmen stood by on the Royal Yacht *Britannia*, which was moored at Holyhead. At Abergele, Denbighshire, a man was killed in a gelignite explosion. In Cardiff six sorters narrowly escaped when a time-bomb exploded at a post office. It was the fourth bomb incident in four months. Telegraph wires running alongside a railway track to Caernarfon were found to have been cut.

Just as fervent Muslims are angered by dilution of their culture, so were the Welsh. Territory in Wales was flooded to provide water for distant English cities. Use of water grows with wealth – for domestic washing machine, dish-washers, garden sprinklers, more bathrooms. Then the richer English bought second homes in Wales, driving up prices so that young local people could not afford them and had to move away. The Welsh language suffered when they went. English second homes were torched. The closure of railway lines under the Beeching plan, then the shutting of post offices, small schools and hospitals, were meant to concentrate resources elsewhere, where they would pay. The decimation of bus services, as with with trains, made travelling more difficult. The Welsh identity was threatened. Revolution through the ballot box – the growth of nationalism – resulted. The Welsh spirit thrives, led by the Welsh assembly.

If the Welsh were under such pressure, were others as well? Is their experience relevant to the causes of terrorism around the world and thus, indirectly, to restrictions placed on British people? At Speakers' Corner, in London, Black Power orators I talked to found the example of Wales entirely relevant. The Black Power movement – or 'black nationalism' as it was sometimes called – was also about identity and the threat to it. Malcolm 'X', whom I met over lunch and talked with during his visit to London before his assassination, told me he had abandoned the name he was given at birth because it was imposed on an ancestor by a slave owner. The 'X' was an assertion of identity.

We have seen earlier in the book how more extreme black power supporters talked rhetorically of putting out the eye of Western capitalism in London and New York. They had felt their identity and well-being threatened by US-led, white, Western society. In certain crucial ways their message was not much different from that of Islamist extremists, who really did attack the eye of the capitalist white octopus in London and New York.

There have been many instances of threats to identity and reaction against them over the last fifty years. They form a tidal wave around the world. There are other examples of action against the US.[5]

In Brazil, Josquin Câmera Ferreira, leader of National Liberation Action, was firmly against US landowners 'who had kicked Brazilians off their land'. In 1962 forerunners of the Tupamaros occupied the offices of an American sugar company, CAINSA, in Uruguay, then marched on the presidential palace with radical students carrying crude effigies of Uncle Sam. Nationalism is always a force to be reckoned with.

Venezuela, Guatamala, Malaya, Colombia, Georgia, Australia and even Switzerland have all experienced tribal or nationalist resentment. Territorial demands led to an explosion that wrecked a Swiss army munitions dump on 16 July 1972. Extremists wanted a separate canton for Jura, which is French speaking and Roman Catholic, and which was administered by the Protestant and German-speaking Canton of Berne. The English planning authorities may find that territory is a dangerously emotive issue if development is more arbitrary under new proposals and democracy neutered.

President Hugo Chávez, of Venezuela, told his troops to prepare for a guerrilla war against the United States if it invaded.[6] He claimed it was already trying by non-military pressure to oust his socialist government and gain control of the country's massive oil reserves.

One of the most persistent internal struggles is in Sri Lanka. The rebellious Tamils were bitter about economic reforms in the late 1970s which meant farm workers lost money they needed to live on. Discrimination against unemployed Tamil youth angers them.

They assert their identity in response to the threat to it – the golden rule of ethnic and religious struggle. The Sinhalese in Sri Lanka comprise some 75 per cent of the population. Most are Buddhist and speak Sinhala. The minority Tamils form about 16 per cent. Tamil is their language and they are usually Hindu. Tamil Tiger recruits each got a cyanide capsule to wear round their necks – the means to martyrdom if captured or if injured in a suicide attack.

Israel defends its identity to the death, and the Jews are great survivors of the many pogroms against them. Their rituals, symbols, language and territory help to bind them. Yet a fundamentalist Muslim, who said his family had lived on the Mount of Olives for centuries, worked with the Israeli tourist organisation. He took a party of Christians around holy sites and showed an indentation in a rock which, he said firmly, was the footprint of Christ when he ascended into heaven.

Over the centuries the Chechen people in the Caucasus have fiercely defended their identity, fostered by territory, distinctive language and the Muslim religion. This gives added force to conflict between separatist forces and Russia. The break-up of the Soviet Union and Yugoslavia allowed ancient tribal peoples to demand independence. August Voss, First Secretary of the Communist Party in Latvia, wrote in the June 1972 issue of *Political Self Education* of the need to wage a 'resolute struggle' against all forms of nationalism. He was fighting attempts to 'destroy the monolithic unity of the Soviet people'.[7]

The word 'monolithic' is a clue to one of the pressures against which nationalism is asserted. Nationalism is at one level an emotional and intellectual defence against the pressures of uniformity which threaten to obliterate a separate identity. In Provence the poet Mistral urged his followers to prevent their culture from being engulfed and overwhelmed by the all-pervading standardisation of the modern world.

The example of the double minority in Northern Ireland is familiar, but the same basic rule applies. Territory is delineated fiercely and has been fought over. Religion is a catalyst. A United Ireland would pose a threat to the identity of the Unionists, and the Roman Catholics long felt a need to defend themselves against the Protestant majority.

The banners, anthems and folk songs which inspire tribal groups are also to be seen and heard at football matches where fans are separated into their territories. Scarves and replica team shirts worn by them are what in another world might be called heraldic symbols. There is nothing more tribal than 'Land of my fathers' sung by the crowd on Welsh national sporting occasions. A group of Gloucestershire rugby fans from the Forest of Dean was chanting 'timber, timber, timber' in support of their team. When I asked why, they explained, as if it ought to have been obvious: 'Nelson's ships were made of our oaks.'

A failure to understand the motivation for territorial, ethnic or religious fervour can lead to disastrous mistakes. No-one, surely, can now believe it was a good idea to invade Iraq without thinking through the consequences and preparing for them. The Shias and the Sunnis, outraged by the attacks which extremists within each faction makes on the other, are a classic example of the hatred that violation of territory and religious symbols can bring. (And similar mistakes have been made in Afghanistan.)

Withdrawal from Iraq would diminish anger towards Britain among Muslims and provide a chance for less mutually distrustful relationships with them in Britain. Partition produced much bloodshed in fanatical religious clashes on the Indian sub-continent, but there are those who would consider partition for Iraq. There has been devolution of responsibility in Wales. Northern Ireland and Scotland, but there cannot be territory separately for Muslims in Britain, who have little enough of it here outside the mosque. However, they can be equal citizens in a free country, restrictive though the response by the government to the population over terrorism has sometimes been. Muslim dress should have the same status as the Scottish kilt, which, of course, covers essentials and leaves the face visible.

Indulgence towards a minority while respecting the national ethos is difficult to manage, but a formula was found by Roy Jenkins, former Home Secretary, on 23 May 1966. He defined integration as 'not a flattening process of assimilation but as equal opportunity accompanied by cultural diversity, in an atmosphere of mutual tolerance'.

There may be more going for such an ideal today than might be thought from the gloomy surveys showing the amount of support in the Muslim community for bombings. The Jenkins ideal was given up-to-date relevance by a far-sighted Gallup report, which had the title: *Beyond Multi-Culturalism vs. Assimilation*.[8] The debate about whether multiculturism was to be encouraged has resulted from the perceived separateness of the Muslim community. Many think it is a mistaken government policy. The eye-catching features of the Gallup report have already been published, as will have been seen earlier in this book. The report itself could well form part of a reassessment of policy. It is by Dalia Mogahed, senior analyst and executive director for Gallup's Center for Muslim Studies.

The study of Muslims in London shows that identification with one's religion and with one's nationality are not mutually exclusive. While most (69 per cent) strongly identified with their faith, a majority (57 per cent) also strongly identified with their country. But being strongly religious did not automatically mean they had been radicalised.

> London Muslims were as likely as the British public overall to condemn terrorist attacks on civilians and were slightly more likely than the general public (81 per cent vs. 72 per cent) to find unequivocally no moral justification for using violence for a 'noble cause'. Views may differ outside London.
>
> Also defying conventional wisdom, a high level of religiosity among London's Muslims did not translate into a desire to segregate themselves.[9]

London Muslims were ten times as likely to express positive views of Christians, while the public is roughly as likely to express positive as negative views of Muslims.

One of the issues which can cause friction is the co-existence of cultures. Most British people (62 per cent) say minorities must be more flexible to blend in with the majority. However, most London Muslims (54 per cent) believe the majority should do more to accommodate minorities' religious customs.

It is in this respect that Roy Jenkins's formula offers a middle way, if political and religious leaders care to use it. If it were recognised that, as this chapter shows, religion is a key part of identity and that it can be asserted if threatened, then less pressure on Muslims might improve race relations and the prospect for peace. The Gallup report shows that there is more goodwill to build on than pessimists have thought. It is difficult to square with other surveys, reported earlier, which are more alarming about potential Muslim support for terrorism.

Scapegoating and harassing the Muslim community will do more harm than good. Raids such as that at Forest Gate can be seen as even more disastrous, given the poll's findings. The raid was a threat to Muslim identity, which can be emotive. The key to peace is the fine judgement that has to be made between vigilance and action to prevent terrorism on the one hand and, on the other, the way the police have traditionally had of exercising discretion. It is an officer's greatest power – knowing whether to act or not. It has become fiendishly difficult because an officer has so many nationalities to deal with. It is hard to pick up signals when arm gestures and shoulder shrugging have their own and different meanings. The power of discretion should not be undermined by bureaucratic targets always demanding measurable results.

To say the police are 'institutionally racist' is superficial. They, too, are a tribe, with long-service families providing stability and experience. As we have seen they have their own jargon and folk memories. They refer to a book on the laws they have to enforce as 'the Bible'. Part of their conflict in the 1970s with young black people was over who controlled the streets – territory, after all. Police, too, assert their identity in response to a threat to it, and they have to be allowed to have one – an identity, that is. Pride in the service is part if it. But enforcing the law requires knowledge of people, and a radical restructuring is needed to get police away from form-filling, to pour more of them on to the streets and allow them to get to know communities better.

The weakness of government strategy to deal with radical Islam in Britain is that it is being conducted from the top down. *The Times* carried a headline on 30 August 2007: 'New anti-terror chief is building elite team'. The story referred to a senior diplomat. He had already built up a staff of 100 civil servants at the Home Office to help him to mastermind the Government's counter-terrorism strategy and find ways to prevent young Muslims from becoming radicalised into suicide bombers. A further 100 civil servants were being recruited. 'Elite' is probably the wrong word.

I wonder how many of the team have learnt, like me, how to roll up a chapatti into a funnel, using it to eat with, scooping up the curry. And just as important would they know the hygiene customs associated with it? And how many of them have slept in a Pakistani lodging house or been asked by young Asians what to do when conflict loomed? Or been with Muslim men when they ended their Ramadan fast in rough old Tiger Bay? Or been to mosques in, say, London, Istanbul and Jerusalem? Of course, some of them may be elite Muslims, but if I had been seen as part of an elite I would not have got far in my own quest to understand what was going on.

The need is to convince young Muslims of the attractions of integration, as put forward by Roy Jenkins.

Foreign policy forays need to take into account more the international effect of what Marshall McLuhan, a guru of his time, years ago called the 'global village'. The whole world sees on television instantaneously what Britain is doing forcibly against terrorism, and what police and MI5 do here reverberates abroad. The difficulty of dealing with extreme Islam is that, although it has a distinctive religion, its territory is not always so clearly, narrowly, exclusively and tribalistically defined as, say, the Basques'. Islam, like Christianity, does not think of itself as confined by boundaries. However, bad strategic planning in dealing with territories like Iraq, which Islamists call their own, can be disastrous.

Realpolitik and a search for common interests are needed in tackling entrenched positions, as when America and Iran tentatively discussed Iraq in May 2007. Extremists treat Islam as a religious ideology. America and Britain have dealt with an ideology before, in Soviet Russia. The old world of diplomacy needs to re-assert itself with ideas like 'spheres of interest' or even 'a balance of power'. The ultimate power in diplomacy was defined to me by an Indian diplomat as 'letting the other fellow have your own way'.

We haven't seen much of that in the shock and awe of the attack

Notes

Chapter 1   Enemies Within

1. *Guardian*, 28 January 2005
2. Liversidge v Anderson (1941) 3 All ER 338
3. Commons Hansard Col 136WS, 7 March 2007
4. Lords Hansard Col 322, 8 March 2007
5. *The Times*, 28 March 2007
6. *Daily Mail*, 10 March 2007
7. *The Times*, January 2006
8. BBC Dimbleby Lecture given by Sir Mike Jackson, 6 December 2006
9. Michael Rose, *Washington's War* (Weidenfeld & Nicolson)
10. *Mail on Sunday*, 14 October 2006
11. British Medical Association conference, 14 June 2007
12. Alan Greenspan, *The Age of Turbulence: Adventures in a New World* (Allen Lane)
13. *Interstate*, 1975/76, Department of International Politics, University College of Wales

Chapter 2   The Police Under Threat

1. Central Bureau of Investigation, Government of India, Annual Report, 2005

2. National Policing Board, 28 November 2006
3. *The Times*, 16 December 2006
4. Peter Clarke, 24 April 2007
5. *Observer*, 11 June 2006
6. *FT.com*, 11 June 2006
7. *Daily Mail*, 12 June 2006
8. Televised news conference, 21 August 2006
9. *The Times*, 13 October 2006
10. *Mailonline*, 16 June 2007
11. *The Times*, 13 October 2006
12. Agencies, *Guardian Unlimited*, 12 October 2006
13. *Daily Mail*, 13 October 2006 and 15 June 2007
14. *The Times*, 23 August 2007
15. *The Times*, 16 April 2007
16. *Recruiting Muslim Spies*, BBC Radio 4, 18 December 2007
17. *Sunday Times*, 23 July 2006
18. Peter Evans, *Prison Crisis* (Allen & Unwin)
18. *The Times*, 23 December 2006
20. http://police.homeoffice.gov.uk/police-reform/policing-improvement-agency/
21. *The Times*, 15 May 2007
22. David Cameron, John Harris Memorial Lecture, 10 July 2006
23. *Telegraph.co.uk*, 25 June 2006
24. *Observer*, 16 January 2005
25. Peter Evans, *The Police Revolution* (Allen & Unwin)
26. *Independent*, 20 July 2007

Chapter 3   Security Services Win Power

1. *Sunday Times*, 19 December 2004
2. *Sunday Times*, 19 December 2004
3. *Mail on Sunday*, 11 June 2006
4. Prime Minister's Questions, *Guardian Unlimited*, 18 January 2006
5. *Daily Mail*, 22 February 2008

6. *Sunday Times*, 16 October 2005
7. Conservative policy group, 26 July 2007
8. Intelligence and Security Committee
9. *The Times*, 5 January 2006
10. *The Times*, 28 December 2005
11. *Timesonline*, 7 May 2005
12. *Telegraph.co.uk*, 14 September 1999
13. *Guardian*, 2 June 2003
14. BBC News, 9 August 2006
15. MI5 website. Dame Eliza Manningham-Buller, The Hague, 1 September 2005
16. Stella Rimington, *Open Secret* (Hutchinson)
17. *Mail on Sunday*, 9 July 2006
18. *The Times*, 20 February 2007
19. *Report of the Interception of Communications Commissioner for 2005–6*. Ordered by the House of Commons to be printed, 19 February 2007
20. House of Lords Hansard Col 1034
21. *Guardian*, 9 July 2005
22. *Mail on Sunday*, 14 January 2007
23. *Guardian*, 9 January 2007
24. *Timesonline*, 17 February 2007
25. Sir Stephen Lander, Centre for Crime and Justice Studies, 13 February 2007
26. SOCA Annual Report, 2006–7
27. *The Times*, 19 May 2007

Chapter 4   Spying on Princess Diana, MPs and Journalists

1. *The Black Man in Search of Power*, *The Times* News Team (Nelson)
2. *The Times*, 10 June 2002
3. *British Journalism Review*. Reprinted in the *Guardian*, 12 June 2000

4. *The Times*, 22 February 2005
5. Peter Wright, *Spycatcher* (Heinemann Australia)
6. *Observer*, 18 August 1985
7. Mark Hollingsworth and Richard Norton-Taylor, *Blacklist: The Inside Story of Political Vetting* (The Hogarth Press)
8. Richard Norton-Taylor, *Guardian*, 22 May 2003
9. Ken Wharfe and Robert Jobson, *Diana: Closely Guarded Secret* (Michael O'Mara Books)
10. *The Times*, 10 January 2008
11. BBC News, 12 February 2008
12. *Guardian.co.uk*, 20 February 2008
13. Annie Machon, *Spies, Lies and Whistleblowers* (Book Guild)
14. Ken Livingstone, Hansard, 10 January 1996, Col 286
15. House of Commons Hansard, 2 November 1998, Col 628
16. *Guardian Weekend*, 8 September 2001

Chapter 5   Judges Under Attack

1. *Daily Mail*, 1 August 2006
2. *Independent.co.uk*, 1 November 2007
3. *Guardian*, 25 May 2007
4. Lord Phillips of Worth Matravers, Singapore Academy of Law, 29 August 2006
5. Report by Mr Alvaro Gil-Robles, Commissioner for Human Rights, on his visit to the UK, 4–12 November 2004
6. Michael Burleigh, *The Third Reich: A New History* (Macmillan)
7. Sky News, 26 January 2007
8. 10 Downing Street, 26 January 2007, and other sources
9. Peter Evans, *Prison Crisis* (Allen and Unwin)
10. *The Times*, 23 April 2007
11. BBC News, 22 May 2007
12. *Guardian*, 23 May 2007
13. BBC2 Newsnight, 26 January 2007
14. Magistrates' Association, January 2007

15. Magistrates' Association, January 2007
16. Department of Constitutional Affairs review, July 2006
17. Sky News, 6 June 2007
18. Dominic Grieve

Chapter 6   Despotism By Stealth

1. *The Times*, 16 February 2006
2. *The Times*, 21 February 2006
3. John Reid speech to think tank Demos. BBC.co.uk/ News/politics, 9 August 2006
4. Dame Eliza Manningham-Buller speech, The Hague, 1 September 2005
5. *Observer*, 23 April 2006
6. BBC News, 12 December 2006
7. Press Association/*Guardian*; BBC News, 22 February 2007, *Gulf Times*, 16 February 2007
8. *Mail on Sunday*, 26 May 2007
9. BBC News, 1 December 2006
10. *Guardian*, 25 April 2006
11. Michael Burleigh, *The Third Reich: A New History* (Macmillan)
12. *Daily Mail*, 23 December 2006
13. BBC News, 10 November 2006
14. *Daily Mail*, 11 November 2006
15. Terrorism Act figures, 11 August 2006
16. Report of the Interception of Communications Commissioner for 2005–6
17. Report of the Interception of Communications Commissioner for 2005–6

Chapter 7   The Subverting of Britain

1. Edward Luttwak, *Coup D'État* (Harvard University Press)
2. Lord Wilson, March 2007
3. *Daily Mail*, 10 March 2007
4. Peter Wright, *Spycatcher* (Heinemann Australia)
5. *Daily Mirror*, 10 May 1968
6. *The Times*, 13 May 1969
7. *The Times*, 9 December 1969
8. *Observer*,15 December 1968
9. *The History of The Times, The Thomson Years* (Times Books)
10. *The Times*, 1 January 1969
11. *The Times*, 30 December 1968
12. *The Times*, 30 March 1981
13. *The Times*, 7 August 1987
14. Sir Robert Mark, *In the Office of Constable* (Collins)
15. *The Times*, 8 January 1974
16. *The Times*, 5 August 1974, referring to Brigadier Frank Kitson, *Low Intensity Operations* (Faber and Faber)
17. *The Times*, 16 August, 1974
18. *The Times*, 4 September 1974
19. *The Times*, 5 September 1974
20. *The Times*, 8 January 1974
21. Peter Wright, *Spycatcher* (Heinemann Australia)
22. *MI5, The Security Service* Third Edition. (The Stationery Office)
23. Ben Pimlott, *Harold Wilson* (HarperCollins)
24. *The Times*, 10 October 1996
25. Mark Hollingsworth and Nick Fielding, *Defending the Realm: Inside MI5 and the War on Terrorism* (André Deutsch)

Chapter 8   Watching The People

1. *Timesonline*, 28 September 2007
2. *Independent*, 22 December 2005

216

3. Poll commissioned by *Computer Weekly*, *E-health Insider*, *The Guardian* and GPs. Computer Weekly.com, 20 November 2007
4. *Telegraph.co.uk*, 29 May 2008
5. *The Times*, 13 February 2007
6. *Guardian*, 31 December 2007
7. *Guardian*, 5 January 2006
8. *Daily Mail*, 23 May 2007
9. *Daily Mail*, 11 December 2006
10. M Gill and A Spriggs, *Assessing the Impact of CCTV* (Home Office Research, Development and Statistics Directorate)
11. *Daily Telegraph*, 21 February 2007
12. BBC News, 17 November 2005
13. *The Times*, 2 October 1970
14. *Timesonline*, 9 November 2006
15. *New Statesman*, 12 August 1988
16. *Guardian*, 30 May 2001
17. Surveillance Studies Network, a charity spreading research internationally
18. *The Times*, 16 January 2008
19. BBC News, 10 March 2006
20. BBC News, 10 March 2006
21. *Guardian*, 3 May 2006
22. *Daily Mail*, 12 October 2006
23. *Mail on Sunday*, 9 September 2006
24. *The Times*, 19 July 2006
25. Liberty statement
26. Harry Snook, *Crossing the Threshold* (Centre for Policy Studies, April 2007)

Chapter 9 Torture – A War Crime

1. Dame Eliza Manningham-Buller, 20 September 2005
2. Dame Eliza Manningham-Buller, 20 September 2005
3. BBC News, 12 December 2005

4. Law Lords, 8 December 2005
5. House of Commons Library, Extraordinary Rendition, Standard Note SN/1A/3816 by Adèle Brown, last updated 23 March 2006
6. BBC Monitoring, 19 May 2005
7. Alleged Secret Detentions in Council of Europe Member States, Information Memorandum II, Committee on Legal Affairs and Human Rights, paragraph 88, January 24 2006
8. House of Commons Library, Extraordinary Rendition, Standard Note SN/1A/3816 by Adèle Brown, last updated 23 March 2006
9. Law Lords, 8 December 2005
10. BBC News, 23 December 2005
11. *Guardian*, 14 February 2007
12. *Observer*, 11 December 2005
13. *Guardian*, 15 February 2008
14. Channel 4 News, 6 December 2005
15. BBC News, 17 December 2005
16. Council of Europe, Dick Marty, 13 December 2005
17. *Mail on Sunday*, 10 June 2007
18. BBC News, 13 December 2005
19. *Daily Mail*, 21 February 2008
20. *Washington Post*, 3 July 2005
21. *Illegal CIA Activities in Europe*, European Parliament, 14 February 2007
22. *Reprieve*, Briefing from Clive Stafford Smith, Legal Director, 5 April 2007
23. Birnberg Peirce & Partners, 27 March 2006. Exhibits disclosed to clients in judicial review proceedings, with the consent of the Foreign and Commonwealth Office
24. Amnesty International UK, 5 April 2007
25. Programmes on torture broadcast on 28 February, 1 and 2 March 2005 on Channel 4
26. Birnberg Peirce & Partners, 27 March 2006. Exhibits disclosed to clients in judicial review proceedings, with the consent of the Foreign and Commonwealth Office.

27. *Intelligence and Security Committee. Rendition.* (The Stationery Office, Cm 7171)

Chapter 10   The London Bombers Free to Kill

1. *Report of the Official Account of the Bombings in London on 7th July 2005* (The Stationery Office), used as a source for relevant items in this chapter
2. *The Times*, 8 July 2005
3. *Observer*, 2 October 2005
4. *Observer*, 2 October 2005
5. Intelligence and Security Committee. Report into the London terrorist attacks on 7 July 2005
6. CBS News, 18 August 2005
7. *Report of the Official Account of the Bombings in London on 7th July 2005* (The Stationery Office)
8. *Sunday Times*, 14 May 2006
9. *Sunday Times*, 14 May 2006
10. Letter from Peter Evans to the Intelligence and Security Committee, 16 May 2006
11. Hansard, 11 July 2006, Col 1323
12. *Observer*, 14 May 2006
13. *MI5, The Security Service*. Third Edition (The Stationery Office)
14. *Londonistan*, Melanie Phillips (Gibson Square Books, 2006)
15. *Security, Terrorism and the UK* (Chatham House and the Economic and Social Research Council, 18 July 2005)
16. Hansard, Col 1035
17. *Daily Mail*, 8 May 2006
18. *Sunday Herald*, 30 September 2001
19. *Observer*, 30 December 2001
20. *The Times*, 22 August 2007
21. Colin Powell Testimony to Congress, Senate Governmental Affairs Committee, 14 September 2004
22. *Intelligence and Security Committee Annual Report*, 2004–5

Chapter 11   'Not the Whole Truth': MI5's Alibi

1. BBC News, 30 April 2007
2. *Daily Mail*, 30 April 2007
3. *The Times*, 1 May 2007
4. *Daily Mail*, 30 April 2007
5. *Daily Mail*, 30 April 2007
6. *Daily Mail*, 30 April 2007
7. BBC News, 30 April 2007
8. *Daily Mail*, 30 April 2007
9. *Sunday Times*, 6 May 2007
10. BBC News, 30 April 2007
11. Charles Clarke, quoted by Rachel North, *Guardian Unlimited*, 30 April 2007
12. *Guardian Unlimited*, 30 April 2007
13. House of Commons, Prime Minister's Questions, 30 April 2007
14. BBC News, 30 April 2007
15. *Guardian*, 3 May 2007
16. *Guardian*, 3 May 2007
17. *Guardian*, 1 May 2007
18. *Intelligence and Security Committee. Report into the London Terrorist Attacks on 7 July 2005,* May 2006
19. BBC News, 1 May 2007
20. *The Times*, 1 May 2007
21. *Guardian Unlimited*, 30 April 2007
22. *Guardian*, 3 May 2007
23. BBC News, 2 May 2007
24. *Sunday Times*, 4 April 2004
25. *Telegraph.co.uk*, 2 May 2007
26. *Guardian*, 12 July 2007
27. *Timesonline*, 11 July 2007
28. *Timesonline*, 5 November 2007
29. *Timesonline*, 20 November 2007
30. *Guardian Unlimited*, 20 November 2007
31. *The Times*, 11 July 2007

32. *The Times*, 11 July 2007
33. *Guardian*, 12 July 2007
34. *The Times*, 11 July 2007

Chapter 12   Bin Laden – a Force in British Politics

1. *Declassified Key Judgements of the National Intelligence Estimate 'Trends in Global Terrorism: Implications for the United States'*, April 2006
2. George Kassimeris (ed), *Playing Politics With Terrorism: A User's Guide* (Columbia University Press, 2007)
3. *Attitudes of Young Immigrants* by Peter Evans (Runnymede Trust, 1971)
4. *Al-Jazeera*, 30 October 2004
5. *Al-Jazeera*, 18 January 2006
6. The 9/11 Commission Report. Final Report of the National Commission on Terrorist Attacks upon the United States.
7. MI5 website, *Timesonline*, 28 July 2005
8. BBC News, 2 September 2005
9. Leak to *New York Times* of Joint Terrorist Analysis Centre (JTAC) assessment, 19 July 2005
10. *Observer*, 28 August 2005
11. ITV, 4 March 2006
12. Thomas E Madden (ed) *Crusades, The Illustrated History* (Duncan Baird Publishers, 2002)
13. Zalmay Khalilzad, 7 March 2006

Chapter 13   The Doomsday Scenario

1. Address by John Reid at the Royal United Services Institute for Defence Studies, 3 April 2006
2. ANSER Report, 'Dark Winter', 22–23 June 2001
3. Maritime and Coastguard Agency press release, 4 May 2004
4. Maritime and Coastguard Agency press release, 4 May 2004
5. *The Times*, 1 and 3 December 2007

6. Computer Crime Research Center, 8 April 2004
7. National Infrastructure Co-ordinating Centre
8. The Council on Foreign Relations, USA
9. John Reid, 25 April 2007

Chapter 14 Defusing the Time-bomb

1. Channel 4 News, 4 June 2007
2. Channel 4 News, 4 June 2007
3. *Shorter Oxford English Dictionary on Historical Principles* (Oxford University Press)
4. *The New Yorker*, 19 November 2001
5. See also Robert Moss, *Urban Guerillas* (Temple Smith, 1971)
6. *Guardian*, 26 June 2007
7. *Political Self Education*, June 1972
8. *Beyond Multi-Culturalism vs Assimilation*, Gallup Center for Muslim studies
9. *Beyond Multi-Culturalism vs Assimilation*, Gallup Center for Muslim studies

Index

223

Compiled by Indexing Specialists (UK) Ltd., Indexing House,
306A Portland Road, Hove, East Sussex BN3 5LP United Kingdom.